Cold Comfort

Cold Comfort

Colds and Flu: Everybody's Guide to Self Treatment

Hal Zina Bennett

A YOLLA BOLLY PRESS BOOK

Clarkson N. Potter, Inc./Publishers   NEW YORK

Distributed by Crown Publishers, Inc.

Cold Comfort was edited and prepared for publication at
The Yolla Bolly Press, Covelo, California, during the spring and
fall of 1978 under the supervision of James and Carolyn Robertson.
Production staff: Diana Fairbanks, Sheila Singleton, Barbara Speegle,
Dan Hibshman, James Koss, Harris Dienstfrey, Don Yoder,
Phil Speegle, Joyca Cunnan, and Pam Frierson.

Manufactured in the United States of America

Library of Congress Cataloging in Publication Data

Bennett, Harold, 1936-
Cold comfort.
Includes bibliographical references and index.
1. Cold (Disease). 2. Influenza. I. Title.
RF361.B46   616.2'03   778-11240
ISBN 0-517-53593-9   ISBN 0-517-53594-7 pbk.

To Linda
who suffers from my colds
more than I do

Contents

Chapter Five
Virus: Villain or Innocent Bystander?
page 59

Most of us have learned that the mere presence of a virus means that
we are going to get sick. This chapter reveals why this is not so.
The information offered here provides you with valuable knowledge for
taking greater control of your health.

Chapter Six
Self-Treatment
page 75

Here's the nucleus of the book. This chapter tells how you can develop
your own self-treatment program for colds and flu. Here you will find remedies
for relieving symptoms — ranging from Grandma recipes to acupressure.

Chapter Seven
Drugs and Upper Respiratory Infections
page 105

A careful examination of drugs frequently used for colds and flu.
Though some drugs can help you, many can impede your progress toward
health or create uncomfortable symptoms of their own. Covers
everything from aspirin to antihistamines.

Chapter Eight
Creating Health: The Step Beyond Prevention
page 119

Tells you how to take an increasingly effective role in your own health care.
The benefits of this chapter can be measured not only in increased mental and
physical comfort, but also in reduced health costs for you.

Foreword

Hal is an important thinker in modern medicine because he is one of the few people attempting to evaluate what *we all can do* to help ourselves create health. His thought is not prejudiced by the stereotypes and rigidities of long, formal medical training but results from a sincere effort to try to figure out what health and illness are and what each of us can do about them. People in the medical establishment have a way of accepting their view of reality as final and correct; Hal is one of the few people who without rejecting medicine broadens it to include other ways of seeing.

The cold and flu are perfect vehicles for Hal's philosophy of medicine. First, the cold is rather simple compared to, let's say, a rare disease; second, medicine can do little for the cold, although doctors in family medicine spend probably half their time on it.

Like the cold and flu, this book is deceptively simple. The reader will discover that it actually involves a different view of reality than what most of us are accustomed to. It presents health as a relationship with the world—a relationship of balance and harmony with the things we do and the world around us. This is truly the holistic view of healing. It is also the essence of good self-help medicine.

Hal believes in helping people to see science's facts that relate to health—so that everyone can use this knowledge to create harmony and well-being in their lives. In this he is one of the fathers of holistic and self-help medicine.

Thanks Hal!

Mike Samuels, M.D.

When all aloud the wind doth blow,
And coughing drowns the parson's saw,
And birds sit brooding in the snow,
And Marian's nose looks red and raw...

SHAKESPEARE, *LOVE'S LABOUR'S LOST*

Chapter One

If You Have a Cold
or Flu Now

If you have a cold or flu right now, this is the place to begin. The answers you'll find here are brief, but more details are found further on in the book.

If you want relief from cold or flu symptoms, you may wish to turn immediately to the chapter, "Self-Treatment" (page 75). The remedies you'll find there are indexed on page 152.

If you are interested in the total program presented in this book, that begins on page 19, but you will also find the questions and answers that follow informative.

Q: *What can I do to feel better?*
A: Rest, relaxation, and warmth, especially in the first days of an infection, greatly increase the effectiveness of your body's self-healing capacities. Relaxing and making yourself comfortable speeds your recovery and reduces chances of complications. You should be aware that many popular cold medicines can actually slow down the healing processes.

Q: *How long will it last?*
A: Most colds last from two to four days. Flu can last as long as ten days. With a cold, the fever and fatigue, if any, usually disappear in two or three days. With flu, fever lasting up to five days is not unusual. Naturally, the longer the fever lasts, the longer one experiences a sense of fatigue.

Q: *How did I get it?*
A: Cold and flu viruses are carried from person to person in the air we breathe. We also spread viruses by our hands—we cover our faces to cough, viruses cling to our skin, we touch these objects and pick up the viruses. But you should realize that viruses alone don't

cause colds. Lowered resistance to infection, through overwork, stress, and fatigue, can make us more inviting hosts for the viruses.

Q: *How can I tell if I have the flu or just a cold?*

A: Sometimes it's hard to tell, even for a trained professional. But in general, flu tends to come on suddenly — the first symptoms are a dry cough, fever, and profound fatigue. Colds tend to build up slowly, beginning with minor symptoms such as a slight headache or an "out of sorts" feeling, then building up to a runny nose, scratchy throat, and maybe a slight fever.

Q: *Am I contagious?*

A: In the first few days of the infection, you are very contagious, but since this phase begins at least a day before symptoms appear, it is virtually impossible to protect yourself or others from person-to-person spread of the infection.

Q: *Should I see a doctor?*

A: For the person who is otherwise in vigorous health, self-treatment for colds or flu will produce as good results as seeing a doctor.

Q: *Can antibiotics help?*

A: Absolutely not. These drugs have no effect whatsoever on colds or flu. They should be reserved for only the more serious bacterial infections.

Q: *Is flu more dangerous than a cold?*

A: No. Any infection of the respiratory tract can temporarily weaken your normal resistance to other diseases such as bronchitis or pneumonia, but with otherwise healthy people who take care of themselves when they get sick, the body's internal healing mechanisms are quite capable of coping with these diseases within a relatively brief period.

Deaths during flu epidemics are not caused directly by the flu, although the media often make it sound that way. In this respect, doctors speak of the "last straw" theory — for a person who is already very sick, say with a serious heart or lung disease, the flu may prove to be that extra little problem that the already overtaxed body just can't stand. It is literally the last straw. Thus the flu can be a contributing factor but not the actual *cause* of the increased mortality rates during flu epidemics. A cold, similarly, might be the last straw for a person who was already quite feeble.

Q: *What about relapses?*

A: Sometimes, with flu, people feel sick for two or three days and then feel much better and start back to work. A day or two later they're back in bed. In many cases the reason for this is simple. After their fever is gone they feel dramatically better and think they're over the infection, but fever is just the initial stage of the flu — the infection can continue for a number of days afterward. Starting back to work too soon may allow the flu viruses to multiply, often without symptoms for a day or so, causing you, in essence, to return to Go and start all over again.

Probably the best way to guard against a relapse is to give yourself at least a day of rest after the fever is gone. During that day your body will be working full time to reduce the virus population still present in your system. If you feel even better the next day after this day of rest, the chances are excellent that your body is ready to take on the regular demands of your work.

Q: What about flu shots?
A: Fewer and fewer doctors recommend them. Because viruses evolve quickly, developing new strains, a flu vaccine developed the previous year may not be effective for current strains. Moreover, research suggests that vaccines may actually promote the evolution of new strains of virus, and thus the widespread use of flu vaccines should be discouraged.

Q: What causes the discomfort I'm feeling?
A: There are several parts to this answer: (1) Aching and fatigue go with having a fever. (2) Inflammation in your nasal passages and throat is your body's way of preventing the infection from spreading. Unfortunately, it also presses on tender nerves, causing facial pain, headache, and sore throat. (3) A stuffy nose is also the result of inflammation; inflammation causes the nasal passages to be constricted. (4) Sore or scratchy throat is caused by superficial damage to the tissue lining your throat and by substances your body produces for repairing the tissue affected by the cold or flu. (5) Low-level anxiety or depression commonly accompanies a cold or flu. People's personalities vary, of course, but mostly these feelings center on four issues: being under the control of a disease you don't understand; feeling vulnerable as a direct result of the weakened state of your body; feeling that you are unable to complete an important job satisfactorily; worrying that your cold or flu may lead to something more serious. (6) The Blahs are caused, in part, by a combination of the symptoms described above. But even more important is the fact that energy you would normally apply to your everyday tasks is now being automatically channeled to

healing. In its energy demands, healing a cold or flu is like taking on an extra part-time job.

Q: *Are colds and flu seasonal?*
A: Yes, for the most part they are. Colds and flu tend to occur in the winter months. If you have colds during the warm months, they may well be caused by allergies rather than viruses.

Q: *Can colds be psychosomatic?*
A: Yes, but first we should be sure we understand what that term means. Medical research demonstrates that emotional stress causes physical changes which can lower natural resistance to infection. Thus you become more vulnerable to viral infection when you are unhappy, overworked, or under considerable pressure. Yes, a "psychosomatic cold" is a real cold.

Think of your mind and body as a complex, intimately interconnected unit. What affects one part affects the whole. This understanding is the basis of psychosomatic medicine. The popular conception that a psychosomatic disease is "all in your head" is a misunderstanding of a theory of disease and health that treats mind and body as one.

Q: *What does it mean to let a cold or flu "run its course"?*
A: The *course* is the period of time it takes your body to identify the virus, build antibodies, and render the virus noninfectious. You get over a cold not because the virus gets tired of your company and decides to move on to the next person but because your body does some very definite things—it identifies the virus, it synthesizes substances that make it impossible for the virus to spread (sort of like feeding the virus a birth control pill), and it repairs tissue damaged by the infection, which it accomplishes by reproducing healthy body cells at a more rapid rate than usual.

Q: *What about using antihistamines, decongestants, and the other cold medicines advertised in the media and sold in drugstores and supermarkets?*
A: Minimize your use of these drugs. None of them shorten the period you have the infection, and many can cause symptoms of their own. My own experience is that they frequently cause further discomfort and can prolong the period you have a cold or flu.

If you feel you must use an over-the-counter remedy—say to get through an important business meeting without sneezing—ask the druggist for a cold pill that is not—I repeat *not*—a combination of ingredients. Popular cold pills are often a veritable stew of drugs.

The drugs sometimes work against each other and often end up compounding side effects rather then healing the cold or flu. Aspirin continues to be the single, most effective, and, at the same time, the "safest" medication for this purpose—except, of course, for those rare cases where people have an aspirin allergy.

Q: What can I do to reduce the symptoms I have without suffering the negative side effects of cold pills?

A: Turn to the chapter "Self-Treatment" (page 75). From the remedies described there you should be able to pick out one or more—or develop your own—that will bring you the comfort you want.

Q: Is there a clear-cut program I can follow for treating colds or flu when I have them?

A: Yes. That's what this book is about. In the next chapter I tell how *Cold Comfort* will help you do that.

Chapter Two

Is There a Doctor
in the House?

*In this chapter, I provide an overall view of this book and make
some specific suggestions about the best way to use the information
it contains.*

*I also introduce the concept of the "self-practitioner"—sym-
bolized by an imaginary doctor, complete with black bag and perfect bedside manner, which we can all create in our minds. This
self-practitioner is actually a mental tool for "looking from the inside in"—a new concept which is the key to the system of self-help
medicine which this book contains.*

Many books on health offer a few tips for accomplishing whatever it is they promise to do for you. Although it would be nice to be
able to guarantee the reader dramatic results by following a few
simple rules, the truth of the matter is that both the human body
and the viruses that cause colds and flu are more clever than that.

You will find that the aim of this book is more general and more
essential—to give readers sufficient knowledge of their bodies' responses to disease and healing in order to allow them to make informed judgments concerning the diagnosis, treatment, and prevention of illness. I have written the book with an intelligent reader
in mind: that is, for readers who wish to be as well informed about
their bodies as they are about getting from place to place in the
communities where they live.

Unlike the trained medical professional, few of us want to spend
many hours every day learning about disease and healing. But we
do possess an interest in health, and one way or another we regularly collect information which serves that end, sometimes without

our even knowing it. Information comes to us in many ways: from
television programs, books, magazine articles, conversations over-
heard on the way to work, and through our own firsthand
experiences.

·   I believe that within each of us there is a part that is normally
concerned with keeping the total organism healthy. This part of us
undoubtedly serves the physiological process that scientists call
homeostasis — the system that automatically makes adjustments to
keep us healthy when there are changes, even extreme ones, in our
external environment, our exercise pattern, our diet, our sleep pattern, or our stress level. Of course, most of the homeostatic adjustments that keep us healthy are completely automatic — such as
temperature control, heart rate, respiration rate, the rerouting of
blood in our bodies according to need, and so forth — so much so
that we hardly need to give them much thought. But there is another part of this amazing system that is learned and fairly
conscious. This is the part, it seems to me, we assist through the
health information that we collect.

Let's take this point a step further. We learn as small children,
after a few uncomfortable encounters, to avoid hot things. Similarly, we learn to wear more clothes or seek shelter when it is cold,
to reduce our level of physical exertion when the weather is too hot,
and to avoid close contact with people who are sick. Much of this
behavior is learned intellectually, but it ends up serving that
homeostatic system which is so automatic we seldom need to think
of it. I like to think of this health-seeking part of myself as my "self-
practitioner."

For me, the self-practitioner is like an imaginary character
created in a novel or a dream. I know I've fashioned it out of my
imagination, but at the same time it has become a handy repository
for everything I've ever learned about staying healthy. I feel a kinship with this personage, a fondness that is similar to the feeling I
experience when I'm reading a novel with a particularly appealing
character.

It is easy to personify one's interest in health, and I highly recommend it. One way you can do this is by imagining that your self-
practitioner is a doctor who was particularly good to you at some
time in your life; or you might lift a character from a favorite novel,
movie, or play; or the self-practitioner could be a composite of
many characters, real and imaginary, whose personality traits have

persisted in your memory. I've known people who created their self-practitioner simply from their own daydreams.

I'm not suggesting that a self-practitioner is something everyone should develop, but I've found it can be a very effective mental tool for the .storage and retrieval of the vast amount of information about health that we all collect through the years. Many people, myself included, find it fun to create a self-practitioner; some of us even use imaginary dialogues with our various self-practitioners as a decision-making technique. If you ever have any doubts about this technique, consider this — it's part of a tradition as old as the human race, called "talking to yourself." In any case, I will be using the self-practitioner in the discussions that follow as a symbol for individual knowledge, in contrast to the licensed healer we go to an office to visit: the doctor.

THE TECHNIQUES OF SELF-TREATMENT

The success of any program for health depends on two important factors: first, the presentation of solid medical information in language that people with no medical training can quickly understand; and second, the description of techniques that will enable people to apply that information in their lives. Discovering such techniques, however, is not simply a matter of rummaging among the traditional methods of doctors to find those that can be used by nonmedical people. A new set of techniques must be designed for the self-practitioner.

Remember that the doctor is looking at the patient from the outside in, while the self-practitioner is looking from the *inside in*. The tools that work for one will not necessarily work for the other. An obvious example of this is provided in the otoscope, that complicated flashlight doctors use for examining people's ears. Clearly, it is impossible to look into your own ears with this instrument; but asking yourself how your ears feel, or simply being aware of their comfort or discomfort, can accomplish for the self-practitioner nearly the same job as the otoscope in the hands of the trained medical professional.

Other adjustments of traditional medical tools are less obvious. For example, the social role of a doctor is such that he or she is asked to take responsibility for other people's lives — you pay a doctor to "cure" a sore throat caused by a bacterial infection. But a doctor can't follow you around for the next four or five days, advising you what to eat, when to rest, and when to go to sleep. Instead, the doctor must invent something to work in his or her absence. Antibiotics to the rescue!

The situation is very different from the viewpoint of self-treatment. Here it is the patient's knowledge that is important, and it is the patient's ability to take responsibility for his or her own body that constitutes the active ingredients of the therapy. In short, the patient very quickly learns how to make the best use of the body's self-healing abilities — abilities, inherited at birth, which are constantly at work maintaining and restoring good health. These physiological facts, which every doctor studies at medical school, form the foundation of all therapies. For doctor and self-practitioner the knowledge is the same; it is the application of that knowledge which differs.

It is a well-known medical fact that you have, within your body, the capacity to heal most bacterial infections without the aid of antibiotics. If this were not so, the human race obviously would have died off thousands of years ago, since bacterial infections have been around for all human history while antibiotics have come on the scene only in the past sixty or seventy years. What is not known, and cannot be determined by anyone other than yourself, is whether you have the knowledge to treat yourself intelligently while your body is doing the necessary self-healing. In short, as soon as a "patient" begins to participate *actively,* knowledge of one's own body becomes paramount, as does a solid perspective on the meaning of disease and the processes of healing.

In this book I've laid the foundation for you to understand the exact processes that occur in your body before, during, and after a cold or flu infection. Once you've read this book you'll have a broad comprehension of both the infectious process and the healing powers you are born with. Through this knowledge, combined with knowledge you already have, you'll have a solid basis for making decisions about health and taking full charge of your own treatment of colds and flu. As an important bonus, you will discover that your knowledge extends to a new perspective on creating health that goes quite beyond the cold and flu.

At this point you may be asking yourself why you need so much information to treat colds and flu. Do you really have to know exactly how human cells become hosts to viruses? Do you really need to understand how the human immunological system works? Do you really need to know how stress and relaxation influence your body's ability to heal itself? Let me assure you that this information leads directly to the practical applications for both the treatment and the prevention of colds and flu.

The end product of your reading this book will be a program of self-treatment—a program for creating health that you can tailor to your own individual needs. Although this may sound complicated, it is not. When it comes right down to it, you'll find this approach far easier to *do* than to say.

HOW TO READ THIS BOOK

Each chapter begins with a capsule outline of the contents to follow. These short introductions have two aims: to prepare you for what is to follow, and to function as reminders after you have read the book. These paragraphs will be especially helpful if you decide to keep the book on your home reference shelf and return to it for practical assistance at a later time.

Toward the end of the book you'll find two chapters, "Self-Treatment" and "Creating Health: The Step Beyond Prevention." In these chapters, we'll draw together the material and develop specific programs for treating and preventing colds and flu. Going one step further, we'll develop the concept of *creating* health, a system of medicine that borrows from our knowledge of prevention and healing but applies that knowledge in a new way.

Let's begin. In the next chapter, I tell the story of what happens during the full course of a virus infection, from the moment the viruses enter your system to the moment when you are completely well again. This information will give you the foundation for understanding virus infection and, perhaps even more important, for understanding your body's exact mechanisms for healing itself when viral infection occurs.

Chapter Three

What's Going On
in There?

Here is the basis for understanding what happens inside your body when you get a virus infection: how the virus reproduces inside body cells; how the discomfort you feel is not caused directly by the virus but by actions your body takes to heal itself; how your body synthesizes chemical substances to stop the reproduction of viruses; and how your body repairs the damage and protects itself from further infection.

Colds and influenza, most medical authorities agree, are viral infections of the upper respiratory tract. Viruses that can cause these diseases number in the hundreds, although the family of viruses most frequently discussed is the group known as the rhinoviruses. But none of this is very helpful when you have a cold or the flu. At such times there are no words to describe your misery. Words like "stuffiness," "aching," and "malaise" seem academic.

Recently a friend of mine sent me a clipping from a local newspaper that I thought came close to describing the true pathos of those poor fellow humans who have fallen under the influence of The Dread Rhinovirus:

> I can't recall seeing a picture of a rhinovirus, but I imagine it is gray and four-legged, with sharp, flinty hooves and a nearsighted affinity for ramming its bony, pronounced proboscis into things that get in its way, like membranes and nerve endings. . . .
>
> Against it we are defenseless: jeeps stalled upon the veldt. We can only roll body and soul into a little ball against its capricious raging, and wait until it is through with us.

Inaccurate though they may be from a scientific point of view, these paragraphs by Michael Grant in the *Oakland Tribune* describe the experience of having a cold far better than most standard medical textbooks. But looking more objectively at the processes that go on in your body when you have a cold or flu, we see a considerably different picture. In the following pages I describe the full course of an upper respiratory infection, breaking it down into its two predominant phases: the infectious phase and the healing phase.

THE INFECTIOUS PHASE

Scientists have identified thousands of different kinds of viruses, all of which cause slightly different symptoms of disease, everything from a slight throat tickle to poliomyelitis. Those identified as cold viruses number in the dozens, though some researchers speculate that there may be hundreds more which cause cold symptoms but have not yet been identified.

The flu viruses are of three unimaginatively named types: A, B, and C. But these three types are subdivided into many subtypes, which in turn are subdivided into many strains. These strains and subtypes occur with most viruses — a result of the virus's ability to evolve: to adapt to its environment and survive. Hong Kong flu, for example, was classified as type A of a particular subtype and strain.

But what exactly is this mysterious creature we call a virus? What does it look like? How does it live? What does it do to cause us so much discomfort?

Starting in the mid-1700s, medical researchers began exploring the theory that diseases might be caused by "infectious agents" that passed from one person to another. Bacteria, which are hundreds of times larger than the largest virus, were the first infectious organisms to be identified. Mainly because of their size, viruses went unrecognized for many years, even though scientists were able to demonstrate the existence of a disease-causing agent that was not a bacterium. It required the invention of a laboratory mechanism for filtering substances smaller than bacteria before the existence of viruses could be fully established. The rather recent development of the electron microscope has made it possible to identify different strains of viruses.

To get an idea of the relative sizes we're dealing with, let's start with the concept of a human cell. We think of these units as extremely tiny, yet the smallest virus has a volume about one billion times smaller! The size comparison is about like a cockroach sitting on an elephant's back.

Though there are some similarities between human cells and viruses, the human cell is considerably more complex. In this respect, bacteria, which are also complex, are closer on the evolutionary scale to human cells than are viruses. Both human cells and bacteria have a nucleus, the control center of the cell, sending out messages to activate their own life processes and to reproduce. This nucleus, in cells and bacteria, is surrounded by cytoplasm, held in by a thin membrane around the whole. The cytoplasm itself contains organelles that serve a variety of functions in the life of the cell. A virus, however, possesses no cytoplasm; it is similar to a nucleus standing alone. (See Figure 1.)

Some scientists speculate that plant and animal cells may have evolved from organisms similar to the present-day virus. One argument for this theory is that the nucleus of most human cells has the same chemical structure as that of the virus: that is, nucleic acids which are either DNA or RNA. But the similarity between viruses and cells pretty much ends there. Whereas human cells, as well as bacteria, can synthesize fats, carbohydrates, proteins, and certain acids, viruses cannot. In other words, cells and bacteria have complex systems for producing their own energy from outside nutrients; the virus is completely without this capacity.

The relatively primitive structure of the virus is one reason it has been difficult for scientists to find a substance that will kill the virus

  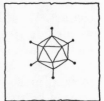

Figure 1: Viruses on Parade. The schematic drawings above represent the shapes and relative sizes of four of the families of viruses that are known to cause colds and flu. They are, left to right: *Adenoviridae, Paramyxoviridae, Orthomyxoviridae,* and *Coronaviridae.* There are further subdivisions and individuals within each family, so what you are looking at is only the tip of the iceberg. If you can pronounce these names on the first pass without stumbling, your cold is getting better.

while not harming the healthy cells of the person in whose body the virus has come to rest. Viruses are completely parasitic. That is, they depend wholly on cells, and sometimes bacteria, to help them carry out their life processes. A virus must actually penetrate the healthy cell, and take up residence inside it, before it can reproduce. And since the virus has already entered cells by the time disease symptoms appear, any medication that would attack the virus would also have to destroy, or at least injure, the host cell or surrounding tissue. The problem of destroying the virus before it enters the host cell is compounded by the fact that the protein sheath and nucleic acids of the virus are almost identical to those of the healthy cell.

The trick for scientists seeking means to destroy viruses while not harming cells is to find something the virus has but the cell does not. Along these lines, a few chemical substances have been found that can dissolve the protein sheath of certain very specific viruses while not attacking the protein of healthy cells. However, no such substances have yet been found that are both effective and safe where common cold viruses are concerned.

Actually, one of the first lines of defense against the viruses that can cause colds or flu is a normal and routine function of your body. There is a "mucosal blanket," made up of fluids and other materials, secreted by glands in the mucosal tissue of your nose, sinuses, mouth, and throat. This mucosal blanket is a little like a conveyor belt, constantly moving through your upper respiratory system and finally emptying into your stomach. It is moved along partly by gravity and partly by microscopic hairs, cilia, that line your nasal passages and throat.

The mucosal blanket, though mostly fluid, contains chemicals produced in your body that can destroy viruses and bacteria on contact. What happens is this: Foreign substances, among which we include viruses, are caught up in the mucosal blanket. Some of these viruses are immediately rendered harmless by the antiviral substances contained in the blanket. Others are carried by the moving mucosal blanket into your stomach, where they are destroyed by the normal acids of your digestive system.

Many people want to know why antibiotics, which work to destroy bacteria, are not effective in annihilating viruses. The reason is that antibiotics do not act directly on the RNA, DNA, membranes, or protein sheaths. Rather, they interrupt the metabolic and reproductive processes of bacteria. Remember that bacteria, like human cells, produce their own energies from outside sources and also reproduce without entering other cells. Viruses depend wholly on host cells to carry out these same processes for them. Thus antibiotics are ineffective against virus infections because the processes they are designed to attack simply don't exist where viruses are concerned.

It is generally believed that viruses which cause colds and flu are carried in tiny droplets of water vapor in the air. Early research, however, demonstrated that the existence of a virus in your system does not, in itself, guarantee that you'll get sick. The fact is that less than 50 percent of both animals and humans tested showed any sign of infection though they'd all received live implants of the same virus. There are many factors to look at in speculating why a virus succeeds or doesn't succeed in causing an infection, but we'll get into that in greater detail later on in this book. Now let's see what happens when the virus does succeed.

Carried by water vapors in the air you breathe, the virus settles in the damp mucosal tissue of your nose, mouth, and throat. In this warm, moist, slightly acid environment, viruses seek out, though probably in a random manner, normal cells on which they depend to carry out their complete life cycles. Not all cells are targets for viruses — some cells resist them, some don't. Natural immunity explains some of this resistance, but medical scientists have not been able to establish why certain cells have an affinity for particular viruses while others do not.

If the virus is lucky — lucky from the virus's standpoint, that is — it finds a host cell and attaches itself to its outer membrane. (See Figure 2.) Here again, the virus's job may not be quite so easy as it seems, because only certain areas of the cell membrane provide an affinity for the virus — an affinity that encourages the virus to attach itself.

The next task the virus faces is entering the cell, which it must do if it is to complete its life cycle. If it simply burst through the cell membrane, the material inside the cell would be destroyed, robbing the virus of its use. Under the electron microscope, it appears as though the cell engulfs the virus. Then a sort of bubble forms inside the cell, made from the cell membrane itself and containing the virus. Behind the bubble the membrane of the cell closes in on itself and thus reestablishes the original integrity of the membrane.

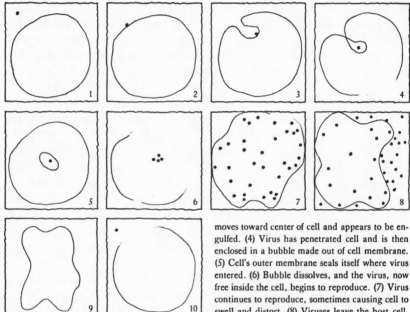

Figure 2: The Romance of a Virus and Cell. This little story could be taking place in real life somewhere in your upper respiratory tract at any time and, if you have a cold or the flu, it probably is. (1) Virus, above left, approaches a healthy cell. (2) Virus attaches itself to cell membrane. (3) Virus moves toward center of cell and appears to be engulfed. (4) Virus has penetrated cell and is then enclosed in a bubble made out of cell membrane. (5) Cell's outer membrane seals itself where virus entered. (6) Bubble dissolves, and the virus, now free inside the cell, begins to reproduce. (7) Virus continues to reproduce, sometimes causing cell to swell and distort. (8) Viruses leave the host cell, now weakened, in search of new hosts. (9) Host cell becomes separated from healthy cells around it and soon dies. (10) The process repeats itself. Remember as you look at these drawings that they are only diagrams and do not begin to suggest relative size. In actuality, a virus is to a cell what a cockroach is to an elephant.

In most cases the virus now sheds its protein sheath and releases its RNA or DNA bundle. The bubble containing the virus then opens and releases the DNA into the cytoplasm of the cell. Once this process is complete, the virus uses the cytoplasm of the cell to reproduce itself, which it does with great speed and in great numbers. From each cell in which this process has been successful, several thousand new viruses may be released — sometimes one at a time over many hours, sometimes all in one rush. The host cell, although not immediately destroyed by the viruses, becomes separated from healthy cells around it. Scientists are not certain about the mechanism that brings this about. Eventually the separated cell dies.

This is the point at which you begin to feel discomfort. You have been unlucky enough to become the home for these viruses. But it is not so much the virus itself that causes your pain and discomfort. The symptoms are actually caused by normal processes your body goes through to heal itself. The discomfort you feel, then, is part of the healing phase of the infection.

THE HEALING PHASE

The discomfort caused by your own body as it goes through the necessary processes to heal a cold or the flu becomes a source of anxiety that most people can appreciate much better after recovering than while they are still suffering its unpleasant symptoms. Complicating the discomfort of the infection is your knowledge, based on past experience, that in most cases pain and discomfort are to be avoided. Ordinarily these feelings signal danger and the presence of a threat to health. And so it is difficult to believe, sometimes, that these same feelings might also be clear proof that your body is doing exactly what it should be doing to heal itself.

The most healthy response to the pain and discomfort of the healing phase of a cold or flu is to acknowledge the discomfort as your body's call for cooperation in the healing process — a call for you to submit to the feelings of lethargy, aching, and general lousiness, and take a very passive role. In other words, rest and relax. Minimize energy spent on activities other than healing.

The process your body goes through to heal a cold or flu requires about the same energy output as hard physical labor. That fact comes as a surprise to most people. But the lesson in all this is clear — we're asking an awful lot of ourselves to continue our regular daily activities while our body is working at the healing process. It is a little like taking on a second job.

Most of the discomfort you feel with a cold or flu is caused by inflammation. For most people the word "inflammation" has come to have a sinister connotation. There is the popular attitude that inflammation itself is a villain and a health hazard, and from this comes the tendency to believe that our bodies are dependent upon antihistamines or other drugs to reduce inflammation. Nothing could be further from the truth.

Inflammation is the human body's natural response to infection. When an injury to tissue occurs — whether it be by infection or by trauma such as cuts, bruises, breaks, or burns — a substance known as histamine is released by the damaged cells. The histamine, in turn, causes tiny blood vessels in the area to expand, bringing an increased flow of blood to the damaged site.

Along with increased blood flow, capillaries (small blood vessels) release fluids into the injured area. These fluids contain large amounts of both protein and a substance called fibrinogen which promotes clotting in areas that might otherwise bleed. The fluids, together with the clotting effect, cause a "walling off" of the injured area, slowing or stopping the exchange of fluids with other areas and preventing the spread of infection.

Discomfort results because the increased fluids press on nerve receptors — sending messages of pain to your brain. Unless you understand that the inflammation is your body's first step in healing the infection, the pain you experience is simply read by your mental computer as it has been programmed to do: Pain signals threat, and the organism should rally its forces to escape that threat. But let's take a closer look at this so-called threat.

With a cold or the flu, inflammation usually occurs in your nasal passages, in your throat, and, if the infection progresses that far, in your sinuses. Inflammation often goes so far as to block the nasal passages, making it all but impossible to breathe through your nose. It can also cause swelling in the throat, producing the characteristic scratchy or sore throat that many people experience with colds and the flu.

Once your body has succeeded in walling off the tissue infected by your cold or flu, a number of things normally occur to hasten the natural healing process. Inflammation, along with the secretions of certain substances by damaged cells, causes your body to increase its production of white blood cells and to stimulate the activity of those already present.

White blood cells are of different types, each performing a slightly different task, but here we need be concerned with only two basic functions of these cells. The first is that some white blood cells surround foreign substances, such as viruses, and digest them, thus rendering them incapable of infecting healthy cells. White blood cells can also surround and digest whatever is left of the tissue damaged or killed by infection, thus cleansing the area of dead tissue that might otherwise encourage bacterial growth.

Other white blood cells produce chemicals that can cause changes in the structure of the virus itself, either making it incapable of attaching itself to healthy cells or destroying its protein sheath so that it cannot enter those cells. This is part of the process known as the immune response.

The immunological system of your body is a system by which, to put it simply, your body is able to recognize the chemical difference between substances or cells that are part of your "self" and those that are "not-self." Within your body, your fluids are being continuously monitored to seek out anything that is not-self. When not-self substances are discovered, your body produces chemicals that make those substances harmless to the self. It is a very complex system, and one that medical scientists have begun to understand only in the past fifty years or so.

When you get a cold or the flu, the virus itself acts as an *antigen* — that is, a not-self substance signaling your immunological system to produce a chemical, called an *antibody*, which renders the virus incapable of harming healthy body cells. In the case of cold and flu infections, antibodies can be produced not only by certain cells in the mucosal tissue of your respiratory tract that are carried by the lymph but also by cells in your blood. Antibodies carried in the bloodstream, as is the case with many flu infections, last much longer than those produced in the mucosa itself.

More serious infections, such as measles and smallpox, signal antibody production in your blood system. When antibodies are produced in your blood, your body can remember how to create the chemicals necessary for protection against that specific virus — for a lifetime in some cases. But when this antibody production occurs in the lymph system (as with colds) protection lasts for much shorter periods of time. To put it in everyday terms, protective substances produced in your bloodstream are more stable than those produced in your lymph system.

These factors help to explain why immunization practices that have proved valuable for protection against, let's say, polio and smallpox do not meet with the same success when applied to the common cold. Vaccination is only slightly more effective in preventing flu infections. Another factor that makes wide protection against the cold and flu difficult is the number of *types* of viruses capable of causing the same symptoms. To be fully effective, an antibody produced by your body must perfectly match the virus you want to destroy. As we've seen, viruses causing colds number in the hundreds, though only three types cause flu; and each new generation of these viruses can change its chemical nature just enough to avoid a perfect match of the antibodies you have already developed in your body.

So you can see that the task your body faces in trying to keep up with the latest cold or flu viruses isn't an easy one. While you are suffering from the miseries of your cold or flu, your body's immunological system is producing antibodies. These antibodies play an active role in helping you to recover from the infection. They also, of course, prevent your immediate reinfection by the same strain of viruses.

Still another factor that researchers believe important in the body's self-healing processes is a substance, called *interferon*, that is produced by cells infected by a virus. Infected cells release interferon, which is carried through the body fluids to healthy cells elsewhere in your body. As the name implies, interferon "interferes." It interferes with the virus's reproductive processes inside the human cell that it tries to invade. The infection is stopped or slowed down because the viruses simply cannot reproduce more of their own kind.

Although scientists do not know exactly how important interferon may be in the human body's defense against disease, experiments have proved it effective in protecting laboratory animals against viral infections. The results of these experiments have been encouraging. Many scientists believe that the study of interferon may well produce the next big medical breakthrough in the treatment of virus-caused infections — and that means everything from the common cold to some forms of cancer.

While we have spoken mostly of the processes the body goes through to rid itself of infection, we have not yet discussed the regenerative processes that are actually being carried out at the same time. During the course of a cold or flu infection, thousands of cells may be destroyed. Most of these are cells that make up the outer layers of the moist mucosal tissue which lines your nose, throat, and nasal passages. When you look at the back of your throat in a mirror and note that it is red or raw looking, what you are seeing is the increased blood flow in tiny capillaries, part of the process to restore tissue that is missing some of its cells destroyed by infection. Your body will replace those cells damaged by infection just as it will replace skin cells injured when you get an abrasion or cut.

Of course, cells are dying and being replaced constantly in your body, so the reproduction of new cells is not by any means a process exclusive to disease. It is known, however, that following injury to tissue through trauma or infection, cells reproduce at a considerably faster rate than they normally do. Healthy cells in the neighborhood of the damaged ones duplicate themselves and continue to do so until the tissue has been fully restored.

The entire process of restoring the damaged tissue will vary according to how much damage has been done. But most medical authorities agree that the restorative processes continue from two to five days after the infection itself has left. Moreover, researchers have demonstrated that most of the cell division necessary for restoring tissue damaged by colds and the flu takes place between midnight and 4 A.M., the period during which most of us are sleeping.

WHAT CAUSES THE DISCOMFORT?

Now that you know how infections occur in your body, as well as how your body heals infections, you may want to relate some of that knowledge to specific discomforts you commonly experience with colds and flu. In other words, what is it about the infection and the healing process that causes the symptoms you suffer? Without this knowledge, we can't truly answer the question "What's going on in there?"

Although it is not known precisely what produces all the symptoms of cold and flu infections, inflammation causing pressure on nerve receptors in the throat, nasal passages, and facial and eye muscles certainly accounts for a lot of it. And lest we forget, this release of fluids is also what causes the runny nose.

It is also known, but seldom mentioned, that the inflammation of a cold or flu can involve, in addition to the sinuses above and below your eyes, a small sinus, known as the sphenoid sinus, which lies deep in the back of the nasal passage. Although most people are aware that swollen sinuses can cause pain above and below their eyes, it is less well known that inflammation of the sphenoid can put pressure on the optic nerve, controlling sight, and on the carotid artery, the main vessel that carries blood to your brain. Dr. Noah Fabricant, in *The Dangerous Cold,* explores these matters in considerable detail.

Research suggests that the sphenoid sinus is not always noticeably affected by cold and flu infections, and in some people it

may never be affected. It also tends to be ignored by doctors
because it cannot be easily seen in a routine examination, and no
routine tests have ever been devised to measure its involvement in
the flu or colds. The shape of nasal passages, the variations in the
sinus structure itself, the differences in people's ability to defend
themselves against infection in this specific area—all are factors
that may determine why one person suffers from sphenoid involvement while others never do.

Sometimes when you get a cold, but more often with the flu, your
body temperature rises. What happens is this: Cells damaged or
destroyed by the infection send chemical signals through your
bloodstream to the master gland in your brain. Secretions from this
gland stimulate glands attached to your kidneys and cause blood
flow to change throughout your body.

It is this change that, in the beginning, leads you to feel chilled
and ache all over. In order to raise the temperature inside your
body, blood is rerouted away from your large muscles and skin surfaces and toward your inner organs. You feel chilled, at first, because the temperature of your skin surface drops. In response to the
chill, you may shiver, an activity that burns calories—and as
calories burn they produce heat. Moreover, in order to feel more
comfortable, you begin putting on more clothes, or moving closer
to the heater, or even going to bed and covering up.

Scientists don't understand exactly how it happens, but it is clear
that there is a part of your brain which controls heat, raising or
lowering your temperature to meet varying demands placed on
your body by the environment, disease, and other influences. In
other words, although we understand how the temperature goes up
—burning calories, putting on warm clothes, moving closer to a
source of heat—it is not known why the brain turns up the internal
thermostat. As your body temperature rises, your metabolic rate
goes up, speeding healing processes. As we'll discuss later, the
increased temperature also makes your body a less inviting place
for the viruses to settle in.

In strict medical terms, the cold or flu is an infection of the nasal
passages and the upper part of the throat only. It does not include,
for example, infection of the sinuses or those regions of your respiratory system below that part of your throat you can see in the mirror. In actual practice, however, there is nearly always some degree
of sinus involvement when you have a cold or flu. Headache, dizzi-

ness, blurred vision, and lack of energy can often be symptoms that indicate sinus infection. Since most doctors classify sinus infection as a complication of cold and flu infections, I've explored that subject in the following chapter: "When Is a Cold Not?"

References

Michael Grant: "A Stampede of Rhinoviruses," *Oakland Tribune,* 17 November 1977, p. 77.
Gay Gaer Luce: *Biological Rhythms in Human and Animal Physiology* (New York: Dover Books, 1971).
Noah Fabricant, M.D.: *The Dangerous Cold* (New York: Macmillan, 1965).

Chapter Four

When Is a Cold Not?

In this chapter, I explain how you can tell if what you have is a cold, the flu, or something else. Several different diseases are discussed here, and each is described in enough detail that you'll be able to make informed decisions about what you have and why. Some of those diseases are ones we worry about getting when we have a bad cold or flu. Others are commonly associated with colds or flu but are actually quite separate. Learning to recognize the differences between colds, flu, and other diseases helps you proceed with the program of treatment that will be most effective for the specific illness you have. There is some discussion of self-treatment in this chapter, but mostly we will be concerned with identifying what's happening to you as a preliminary step toward developing your own treatment program.

Although most of us have no difficulty recognizing the symptoms of an upper respiratory illness when we have one, even the medical profession may have trouble saying with absolute assurance that what you have is a cold or the flu. It is true that laboratory tests of cultures taken from your throat can give positive identification of the kind of virus you have, but doctors rarely do this in everyday practice. What's more important is that the throat culture is out of the question for the self-practitioner. How then do you determine whether you have a cold or the flu? Although not even the best doctors are 100 percent right 100 percent of the time, even with laboratory tests, there are some good criteria by which you, the self-practitioner, can make an educated guess.

COLD OR FLU—WHICH IS IT?

Researchers tell us that cold viruses and flu viruses are completely different organisms. Although they're all viruses, the similarities end there. From what we know about the differences between cold and flu viruses, it seems that most flu viruses have a greater ability to overcome the first hurdles of our defense mechanisms than do most cold viruses. Thus the antibodies and other virus-destroying substances in our mucosal tissue, which are extremely effective against cold viruses, may be less efficient against the flu.

Most physicians say that the presence of chills, fever, headache, generalized muscle aches, and sometimes a feeling of tiredness or even exhaustion are present with the flu to a greater extent than with a cold. On the other hand, sore throat, hoarseness, cough, nasal congestion, and discharge are present with both. It is also said that flu comes on suddenly. You feel great one moment and terrible the next. A cold creeps up on you more gradually.

Most flu infections occur on an epidemic or pandemic scale—that is, infecting a large community, or the whole continent, or even the whole world, at one time. In a sense, flu viruses are much more ambitious than common cold viruses.

As a simple guideline for deciding whether you have a cold or the flu, you would be safe in assuming that you have flu if you answer yes to the following:

> Do you have a *dry* cough?
> Did you feel great yesterday and lousy today?
> Does your head ache?
> Do you have chills and fever?
> Do you have a sore throat?
> Do you ache all over?
> Did you recently hear that the flu was going around?

So what difference does it make, in terms of self-treatment, to know that you have the flu or just a cold? For most people, the greatest benefit of this knowledge will be to reduce anxiety about what it is they have. At first glance this may seem like a small thing. But emotional stress, in this case worrying about what disease you have, can actually inhibit the healing processes.

Moreover, knowing what you have will give you some idea of how long it will take your body to heal. In general, you can usually calculate that a cold will last from two to four days and the flu from four to ten. Many people, when they have colds or flu, get impatient with the length of time it takes to recover. Their impatience may take different forms: returning to regular work routines too soon, getting angry with themselves for becoming sick, or getting worried that the cold or flu, because it is taking so long, is really something more serious. All these factors impose additional stress, and they divert energy from your body's healing processes. But knowing the normal terms for the cold or flu allows you to have a more realistic perspective about the infection and your body's needs for healing it.

MEDIA REPORTS CAN HELP

Knowing something about the media and the medical establishment may seem like an interruption at this point, but bear with me for a moment and you'll soon have a grasp of a simple diagnostic tool that doctors use to diagnose flu.

Health departments keep a careful lookout for infectious diseases that may affect their community. Identifying flu viruses is one of their jobs. Whenever respiratory illnesses appear in great number, cultures are taken from infected people and observed in the laboratory for a number of days. When flu viruses are identified, reports of these findings go out to the community at large. Usually this means no more than releasing the information to the media: to newspapers, radio, and television.

If you were a doctor, you'd probably subscribe to a public health newsletter that reported on various infections within your community. But like most busy professionals you'd probably depend as much on television and radio to learn about the flu as you would the reading of this newsletter. If a patient came to you with symptoms typically associated with the flu, during a time when it had been reported that flu was going around, you would probably make the assumption that this person had the flu. Media reports would be important in your diagnosis. Although this might seem haphazard, consider the fact that to make a more accurate diagnosis, by sending a culture on the virus to the laboratory, you would have to wait up to a week for the results. By the time you had a positive identification of the virus your patient would be well on the way to recovery.

There's no reason in the world that you can't do pretty much as any good doctor does during a flu epidemic. That is, consider your knowledge of media reports on flu as part of your diagnosis of upper respiratory infections.

THE COMPLICATIONS

Now let's look at the complications that can come with colds or flu. Figure 3 shows where the main complications are sited. We'll begin with sinus infections.

Sinus Infections

The symptoms of sinus infection are well known, though not everyone has necessarily learned their meaning. The symptoms are:

Pain or pressure directly *under* one or both eyes
Pain or pressure directly *above* one or both eyes
Aching teeth, especially the upper back teeth, when you have no
  reason to expect dental problems
A sense of having "long" teeth
Slight blurring of vision
Pressure or pain along the upper bridge of your nose, extending
  down each side, close to the corners of your eyes
Pain deep inside your head rather than around your forehead,
  temples, face, and teeth

There are five sinus cavities in your head that can become infected from having a cold or the flu. Two are located above your eyes, two under your eyes, and a fifth, the sphenoid, nearly in the center of your head. (See Figure 4.) The sinuses are like hollow caves in your head, lined with damp mucosal tissue like that which lines your nasal passages and throat. Mucosal cells in the sinus areas produce moisture and antibody substances that then drain into your throat, providing additional fluid to the regular mucosal blanket.

Each sinus cavity has only one route in and out of it—that being the passage through which moisture passes to the throat. Because of the narrow interconnections between the throat and the sinus cavities, it is easy for a viral infection to travel to one or more of these sites. When your sinuses do become infected, the same thing that happens in your nasal passages happens there: The area becomes inflamed and the inflammation causes pressure on nerve

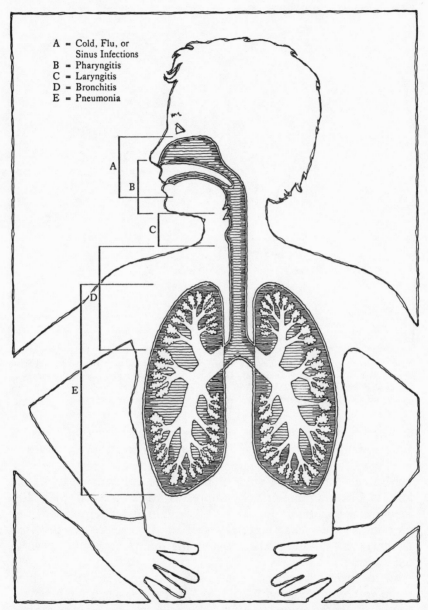

A = Cold, Flu, or
      Sinus Infections
B = Pharyngitis
C = Laryngitis
D = Bronchitis
E = Pneumonia

Figure 3: Where Infections Are Located: This is a map of your respiratory system. Most diseases occur in specific areas of this system, though the borders are not always as clear-cut as they are shown here. Study this drawing carefully. Once you get a clear picture of where specific illnesses occur, you'll have an important tool for diagnosing and treating common respiratory diseases.

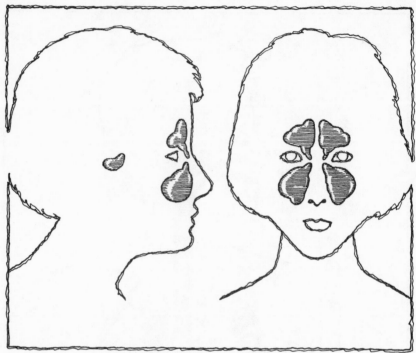

Figure 4: Locating Your Sinuses. This is a map showing the locations of the five sinuses. Any one or even all of them can become infected. When a person has a sinus infection, pressure applied with the fingertips in the sinus areas above and below the eyes will usually cause pain. So that is one way to diagnose sinus infections and even to detect how many sinuses are involved.

endings. Sometimes the nerve endings involved serve other parts of your body: your facial nerves, nerves to your teeth, even nerves to your eyes.

Methods for relief of sinus pain include applying heat, in the form of a heating pad or hot compresses, to the areas of pain. Relaxing your facial muscles, which I'll explain in detail in the chapter on remedies, can also help. A weak tea of cayenne powder (red pepper) can also bring relief, though the spicy taste is not to everyone's liking.

In my own experience, I've found that sinus infections which come in conjunction with colds or flu can be reduced by overcoming the temptation to *sniff* when trying to clear your congested or runny nose. The sniffing causes a suction, deep inside your clogged nasal passages, which tends to draw mucus from your cold up into your sinuses. Gently blowing your nose tends to draw mucus away from these sites. But remember: Gentle blowing is important; hard blowing can also send infected mucus to the sinuses.

It's important to know that nasal sprays, nose drops, and certain other cold remedies can cause nasal and sinus tissue to become inflamed. Sometimes this inflammation is in fact the cause of what you may take to be a sinus infection. Although I discuss this matter in greater detail in the chapter called "Drugs and Upper Respiratory Infections," it is worth noting here that the discontinuation of such drugs may well be your best preventive measure against sinus pain.

Sometimes sinus infections are caused by viruses, sometimes by bacteria. Just because the original infection that led to the sinus infection was viral is no guarantee that the sinus infection is also viral. A sinus infection that persists—that is, which you have even without a cold, and which did not appear along with a cold—may be caused by allergies. A sinus infection that you got along with a cold, but lingers after the cold or flu is gone, may be caused by bacteria.

The reason for knowing this is twofold. First, if sinus infection persists you might want to go to a doctor for treatment. The doctor might recommend antibiotic treatment if he or she suspected bacteria to be the cause. In this case it would be helpful for you to know that the doctor could be quite accurate in suggesting such a treatment; otherwise you might argue that the antibiotics wouldn't help because the original cold or flu had been viral. Second, let's say you had a cold or flu, got better, had a painful sinus infection, and then had an apparent relapse putting you in bed again, this time with a very sore throat. In such a case you might consider the possibility that the sinus infection, as well as the sore throat you had with the relapse, had bacterial origins. A culture by the family doctor might then be in order.

It is not uncommon for a sinus infection to linger on a few days after all the other symptoms of a cold or flu have disappeared. Most people resume their normal routines at this point, probably because they don't associate the sinus discomfort with infection, but a better procedure is to take it slow and remember that your body is still using energy to heal the infected sinuses.

Most doctors can recommend ways to get relief if your sinus infection is particularly painful or persistent. These methods of relief vary from one individual to another but may include hot compresses, antihistamine nose drops, or even antibiotics, if pus and other indications of bacterial infection are present. Never hesitate to use your doctor as a resource for symptoms that puzzle you.

Ear Infections

Like your sinuses, your ears are connected to your upper respiratory system — and thus are vulnerable to infection during or after a cold or the flu. From each of your ears there's a tube, lined with mucosal tissue, emptying into the sides of your throat. These tubes — the eustachian tubes — can become infected and inflamed from the cold or flu, causing pain or a feeling of fullness as pressure builds up in your ears.

Ear infections are more common in children than adults, in part because the eustachian tubes change in shape and size as the person grows, reducing the turns where infection settles, and in part because most children sniff a lot when they have colds, forcing virus-infected body fluids up the tubes.

When medical researchers compared cultures taken inside the ear with cultures taken from the throats of the same people with colds and ear infections, the infectious agents from the two sites were found to be different; a virus caused the cold, while bacteria caused the ear infection in the same person. Apparently, a virus lowers the resistance of the eustachian tubes and the ears; then bacteria already present, but not causing any problems, begin to multiply and cause infection.

Do not expect outward signs, such as draining, when you have an ear infection. Usually the sharp pain as pressure builds up inside the ear is quite a sufficient signal to seek relief. Young children with ear infections will often pull at their ears, signaling the parent that this may be the problem.

Ear infections can be extremely painful, and as a result most people seek relief by going to their physician. Sometimes doctors prescribe antibiotics along with decongestants: the antibiotics to fight infection, the decongestants to reduce inflammation, allowing the eustachian tubes to open enough to drain the ears. Often heat will bring relief, especially if a *warm* heating pad or a hot water bottle is applied to the ear affected. Another treatment offered by doctors is to make a small incision in the eardrum, allowing the infection to drain into the outer ear. Although this may sound a bit

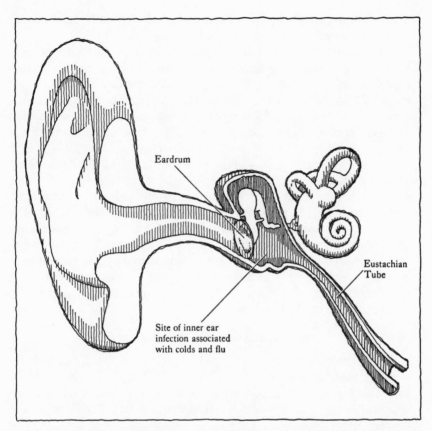

Eardrum

Eustachian
Tube

Site of inner ear
infection associated
with colds and flu

Figure 5: The Human Ear. The drawing above tells the inside story of the human ear. The important thing here is to get a clear picture of where the eardrum is located, since its position generally establishes the dividing line between an *inner* and an *outer* ear infection.

unpleasant, doctors are able to bring fast relief in this way, and they claim a more lasting therapeutic effect, especially for those who suffer from chronic ear infections. The procedure itself is considered simple and painless.

One of my own sons suffered through many an ear infection, going to doctors for antibiotics that never seemed to help. Then we began to apply our own form of treatment. On the preventive side, he learned to blow his nose gently when he had a cold, rather than sniffing, as he'd always done. He also took a gram of vitamin C with each meal and snack throughout the day. We gave him a simple decongestant (not one combined with other drugs) in the morning and at night. During the day an aspirin seemed to be sufficient for reducing inflammation and pain.

We encouraged him to sit upright, or with his head on two pillows, rather than lying down — this helped to keep the ear canals elevated and in a draining position. We also got him to keep his jaw muscles relaxed and loose, encouraged by snacks such as apples, raw carrots, or celery. As the jaw muscles relax, muscular tension around the eustachian tubes is released, in some cases allowing the tubes to begin to open and in all cases increasing blood flow — with all its healing substances — to the general area. For children with a sweet tooth, chewing gum will accomplish similar results. For our son, this combination of techniques has done wonders where antibiotics have failed. However, the medical establishment, for the most part, continues to favor antibiotics or lancing of the ear drum, or a combination of these, in the treatment of ear infections — especially in young children. These physician-administered treatments, it is felt, work quickly and so do not require constant supervision afterwards. It is also felt that the use of antibiotics prevents the spread of bacterial infections.

Constipation, Diarrhea, and Stomach Flu

Three complications — constipation, diarrhea, and stomach flu — affect the digestive system. The simplest, constipation, can be associated with a cold or flu for the simple reason that you are sedentary, and perhaps tense, while you are sick. Ordinarily, the movement of feces through your intestines is aided by exercises such as walking, running, stooping, getting up, climbing stairs, and so forth. Often when people are sick they quite naturally lie down and hence miss their normal exercise. Drugstore cold remedies can also contribute to constipation. Avoid the use of harsh laxatives when this happens. Instead, take a look at the remedies in Chapter Six.

Diarrhea is a slightly more complicated, and certainly less common, occurrence with colds and the flu. Sometimes caused by viruses, the infection can cause inflammation of your digestive organs the way it affects your upper respiratory tract. This attack, of course, is greatly disruptive to the digestive processes and results in loose or watery stools. The major problem with diarrhea is that it dehydrates you. Fluids usually absorbed and used by your body to maintain healthy water levels in tissues, lymph, and blood are emptied from your body through your intestines. So it is important, at such times, to compensate for this loss by maintaining a high fluid intake. Infants who have diarrhea should be checked by a physician; an infant, being much smaller, has far less ability to cope with dehydration than does an adult.

Stomach flu is caused by a virus and is medically the same as diarrhea. There are times when large portions of the population are affected by flu infections that characteristically involve diarrhea in addition to upper respiratory discomfort. As far as treatment is concerned, everything that applies to diarrhea also applies to stomach flu.

Sometimes loose bowels are caused by other things: food poisoning, bacterial infection, reaction to drugs, even fungus poisoning. If you've eaten anything questionable, or if you are taking *any* kind of drugs, even if you have a cold or flu that seems to be causing the diarrhea, don't overlook the possibility that food, or even pharmaceuticals, could be causing your digestive problems. In the chapter, "Self-Treatment," I tell about a number of things you can do to help relieve these problems.

Cold Sores, Cankers, and Fever Blisters

Sometimes, during a cold or flu or soon after, people get small sores on their lips, inside their mouth, or even in their nose. The pain of these sores often seems out of scale to their size. These sores, known medically as herpes simplex or apthous stomatitis, can be caused by a virus that, unlike other viruses, usually prefers a hot environment in which to reproduce. Since these sores seem to appear frequently during a cold or flu infection, it is believed that a lowered resistance, combined with a slightly heightened body temperature, may encourage the viruses to multiply and cause sores.

Although the viruses that cause herpes are extremely common— so common in fact that researchers speculate most of us may have them in our bodies all the time—only certain people seem to be troubled by their symptoms. People who do get these sores report that they appear most frequently when they are under a lot of pressure, or when fatigue or a slight minor illness has lowered their body's resistance, or when they have been in the sun for long periods. These sores disappear in a number of weeks and, like the cold or flu, your body will heal itself and repair the damaged tissue automatically.

If you must be out in the sun when you have a cold sore on an exposed part of your lip or nose, protect it by applying a sun screen ointment, such as that used by skiers and swimmers, since the rays of the sun can aggravate it. In the later stages, these sores sometimes become moist and ooze. Doctors often recommend swabbing the sore with a drying agent or an alcohol solution (70 percent alcohol). Although some experimental work has been done on drugs to help your body heal herpes simplex, their potential side effects are still in question. The use of vitamins and yogurt culture to treat canker sores and cold sores is noteworthy. Read more about this in the chapter "Self-Treatment."

Parainfluenza

Parainfluenza is a viral disease like colds and flu, which we've already discussed, but it is slightly different when children get it because it can lead to the disease called croup, a flu-like disorder that causes a barking cough. It is believed that parainfluenza viruses are extremely common, causing cold and flu symptoms in both children and adults. In children, these viruses can cause illness the year around, although like most upper respiratory infections most viruses occur in the fall and spring seasons. Parainfluenza is usually seen in epidemic-like outbreaks in nursery schools or wherever else large numbers of young children congregate. The symptoms are the same as for most other upper respiratory diseases, and in most cases, with children who are normal and healthy, the disease doesn't develop into croup.

A child who has had a bad cold or flu and shows signs of having to work hard to breathe should have a doctor examine him or her in order to get treatment to avoid croup, bronchitis, or pneumonia. Children with croup have a barking sort of cough that is caused by constricted air passages resulting from the infection. Early treatment of colds or flu is the best preventive measure. Croup requires a physician's help.

By the time children are five or six, they have usually developed at least partial immunity from parainfluenza viruses and other specific viruses which cause complications that need professional medical assistance. Most children have many colds in their early years, and by far the greatest number of these do not result in serious complications. The fact is that getting colds may be one important way our immunological systems learn to protect us from viral infections. So while you are remembering that colds and flu have their mixed blessings, watch your child's colds with an educated eye.

Throat and Chest Complications

Sore throat, tonsillitis, laryngitis, bronchitis, pneumonia — each of these is a specific disorder, but all of them are diseases you can get if your upper respiratory infection starts moving down into your chest. We'll discuss each of these complications individually.

All these diseases can be caused either by viruses or bacteria. The main difference, in terms of treatment, is that viral infections do not respond to antibiotic treatment, while bacterial infections do. Your body is quite capable of healing either kind of infection on its own, of course. But only the bacteria-caused diseases respond when speedy, antibiotic-assisted treatment is desired.

Sore Throat (Pharyngitis). This term refers to an infection in your throat that, like ear and sinus infections, can be caused by either viruses or bacteria. It will help the self-practitioner to know that in diagnosing a sore throat even the most conservative physicians take a moderate approach. That is, a sore throat is considered to be one of the usual symptoms of a cold or flu. In most cases, the same home treatments that apply for cold or flu should be followed.

But is your sore throat just a regular cold or flu symptom or is it the more serious strep throat infection? Strep is a bacterial infection that many doctors like to treat with an antibiotic — not because your body is incapable of healing it without this help, but because strep throat infections have been known to lead to rheumatic heart disease and kidney malfunctions. Thus the use of antibiotics for the strep infection is considered a preventive measure. But this complication is *not* a common occurence: Sore throats are seldom strep infections, and only rarely do strep infections lead to heart or kidney diseases.

Then how does the self-practitioner make a judgment about what kind of sore throat he or she has? Is it a regular sore throat or a strep infection? Consider the following information whenever you're faced with this question.

First of all, ask yourself if you've recently been around people with colds or flu. If you have been, and if you are in the first stages of such an infection, then consider your sore throat to be one of the symptoms of that condition. With a strep throat infection, on the other hand, the person is often aware of only two symptoms: an extremely sore throat and a high fever. There may be other symptoms, such as stuffy nose, headache, and chills, but if the sore throat itself seems the most severe symptom, this may be a sign of strep infection. In examining a patient who has come in with a sore throat, a doctor will pay particular attention to the first symptoms that person reports. If sore throat is the first thing mentioned, the doctor will often take a throat culture and send it off to the lab for identification to rule out the possibility of strep infection.

If the patient is able to get good bed rest and relaxation, the doctor will probably tell him or her to treat the sore throat as a symptom of flu or a bad cold. If good home care is not possible at the time, however, the doctor may prescribe antibiotics. Many doctors, because they do not want to prescribe antibiotics for diseases the body can heal itself, will at least wait until the lab tests are in on the throat culture before writing such a prescription.

In general I follow this simple rule when a member of my family is presented with the choice of taking or not taking an antibiotic: *The less you use antibiotics for minor infections, the more you will be able to depend on them if you ever need antibiotics for major infections.* If good home care is possible, don't use antibiotics for a sore throat you only suspect of being a bacterial infection.

But what if you're faced with something like bronchitis or pneumonia, which we discuss later on in this chapter? The thing to understand here is that a sore throat means you'll be uncomfortable for a few days. That's something you can handle. But the impaired use of your lungs is quite another matter. A lung infection means that every cell of your body will be receiving a reduction in its oxygen supply and a reduction in the removal of the waste gases each cell of your body produces every moment of your life. These are vital services rendered by vital organs, and where these functions are concerned you'll obviously want the most rapid return to health available to you. That is where antibiotics can excel. Much human suffering has been made unnecessary by these drugs.

About the most valuable information for the self-practitioner to know about sore throats is this: They are more the rule than the exception in the early and middle phases of a cold or flu and require nothing more than the home treatments you'd apply in those cases. When fever continues longer than the usual course of the flu, along with severe sore throat, that's the time to consider strep infection, not before.

For the usual sore throat that characteristically accompanies a cold or flu, antibiotics are of no value — the sore throat of colds and flu is a viral infection, and antibiotics only work for the treatment of bacterial infections. Remember also that the usual sore throat which accompanies many colds and flus poses no danger of becoming anything more serious. It is a viral infection your body will heal within a few days.

Mild saltwater gargles, or a small amount of honey dissolved in your mouth from time to time, or slippery elm lozenges (carried by health food stores) can all bring safe and comfortable relief. Stay away from strong-tasting cough drops or ones that have pain-killing properties. These only mask the symptoms; they don't cure anything. The self-practitioner needs to keep in touch with his or her body. After all, you can't take responsibility for something you can't feel! More remedies for sore throat are discussed in the chapter "Self-Treatment."

Tonsillitis. What goes for pharyngitis generally goes for tonsillitis. Both can be caused by either a virus or bacteria, and although many doctors will take a culture before prescribing antibiotic treatment, it is generally agreed that more tonsil infections are caused by bacteria than by viruses. Sore throat and difficulty in swallowing are common symptoms of tonsillitis. Children who have it may not complain of sore throat but may refuse to eat or drink anything because of the discomfort it involves. Unless appetite and the intake of foods are markedly reduced, tonsillitis can be treated as you'd treat other sore throats. Otherwise, especially where children are concerned, a doctor might advise you of other treatment.

Laryngitis. Most people, at some time in their lives, have had the experience of losing their voice during or after an upper respiratory infection. This voicelessness occurs when the lower part of your throat, and sometimes your vocal cords, become infected or inflamed.

Although laryngitis can be caused by either viruses or bacteria, the approach of most doctors is to find out whether or not you have a cold or the flu at the time. If you do, the doctor will probably treat the laryngitis as an outgrowth of it and send you home with the assurance that you will get your voice back as soon as you get over your cold or flu. If, however, the doctor had taken a throat culture and found the presence of bacteria, he or she might assume the laryngitis also had a bacterial origin and treat it accordingly.

Bronchitis. Your bronchial tubes, leading from your throat into your lungs, look like the trunk and major branches of a tree. (See Figure 3 on page 43.) Deep inside your lungs oxygen from the air is absorbed into your bloodstream through bulbous little sacs that look like berries at the ends of the branches; these are called *alveoli*. Bronchitis is an infection involving the larger branches, usually in the area where the single tube, which carries air from your mouth, branches into two parts to carry air to your two lungs; bronchitis doesn't involve alveoli.

A cough and slight backache, along with the other symptoms of a cold or flu, can indicate bronchitis. The cough is usually dry at first but soon brings up some phlegm. Your cough, though annoying, is important to your health since it keeps your air passages clear and helps prevent the infection from going deeper into your lungs. A fever is often present, usually not higher than 101 or 102° F., lasting three to five days. Pneumonia may be present if fever goes outside these limits. If you have bronchitis, it is not unusual for a cough to hang on two or three weeks, even after most of the other symptoms of your cold and flu subside.

It's important to treat yourself well when you have bronchitis and to make full use of all your knowledge and resources where self-treatment is concerned. As an infection goes deeper toward your lungs, there is greater chance of a pneumonia developing—which you want to prevent.

Pneumonia. Unlike most other respiratory infections, pneumonia can threaten basic life processes. It involves the tiny alveoli, deep inside your lungs, where oxygen is absorbed into your bloodstream from the air you breathe and where carbon dioxide, excreted from your blood, is carried into the air and exhaled. Blocking those exchanges means robbing your cells of oxygen (for metabolizing nutrients) and preventing them from getting rid of carbon dioxide.

The symptoms of pneumonia, when coming as a complication of a cold or flu, are often very distinct: sharp chest pains, cough, sudden "shaking" chill, fever rising rapidly to 101 to 105°F. Sometimes nausea and vomiting are present. Doctors will usually recommend complete bed rest and a course of antibiotics. Penicillin is the first choice for fighting pneumonia, but in patients with a history of allergy to this drug, others are used. Bear in mind that if the agent causing the infection is a virus, and not a bacterium, the antibiotics won't help. Your body must do the healing by itself. Complete recovery is usually within two to five weeks, depending on the person's age, general health, and kind of treatment.

Since pneumonia can be serious, even causing death in infants or in older people who are not otherwise in good health, doctors treat the colds and flu of people in these categories with special attention. Prevention of complications is absolutely essential.

The Non-Complication Complication — Allergy

If you have what you believe to be colds the year around, rather than just during the cold and flu season, it may be worth your time to explore the subject of allergies since the symptoms of many allergies are very similar to those of a cold.

An allergy is caused by a substance, either synthetic or natural, which is *not* a virus or bacterium. And yet your immunological system reacts to that substance as though it were a potential disease-causing agent. Your body produces antibodies, and inflammation takes place to wall off the site of "infection." Your symptoms are caused not by the allergenic substance itself, however, but by your body's reaction to that substance.

Where do you begin if you want to determine whether or not some of your colds are actually allergic reactions? Here's a list of potential troublemakers:

House dust, dander in animal fur
Feathers or products with down fillings (jackets, pillows, down comforters)
Kapok (used in filling pillows)
Fungus and fungus spores
Food preservatives (such as sodium benzoate)
Food coloring (especially tartrazine yellow)
Eggs, chocolate, milk, strawberries, cheese

And the seasonal, natural allergenic sources:

Spring: oak, elm, maple, alder, birch, and cottonwood tree pollens
Summer: pollens of grass, sheep sorrel, and English plantain
Fall: ragweed

If you are taking *any* prescription drugs you should ask the doctor who prescribed them if there is any possibility that you could be getting an allergic reaction from them.

Don't overlook over-the-counter drugs, either. Certain of these are known to have significant allergenic potential:

Nasal sprays and nose drops
Cold pills
Aspirins and aspirin substitutes

It may seem ironic that medications which are presumably designed to reduce cold symptoms could also *cause* those symptoms, but it is true. Medical researchers talk of the "bounce back" syndrome with certain medications used to dry nasal passages. After a period of taking them, your body speeds up its production of histamines, and the result is more inflammation and discomfort than with the original symptom for which the medication was taken.

Allergy specialists talk about tolerance levels for people who have allergies. Let's say, for example, that you're allergic to strawberries, house dust, feathers, animal fur, and cheese. Most of the time your body tolerates these allergens. But when tree pollen is added to the list your nose starts running, you sneeze, you cough, and life becomes gruesome.

Understanding this tolerance theory has been extremely important for people with allergies. Here's how you can use it: By going through the list of allergy-causing substances, either the one offered here or a list your doctor can provide, you can use a process of elimination to discover your allergies. This is time-consuming but ultimately effective.

Let's say you have been using a nasal spray frequently and over a long period of time. Suspect this medication as your first allergen. In addition, you work in a dusty office and your roommate has birds. Since it's spring and the streets in the town where you live are lined with maples, you can assume that the air is filled with maple tree pollen.

You can't do much about the trees, but maybe you can reduce the number of allergens in your life so that the tree pollen doesn't bother you. You start by having your office cleaned, but nothing happens right away to your allergy. Next you have your roommate trade the birds for fish. You, of course, have to clean the house and dust carefully to remove all the feathers left behind, but a couple weeks later you begin to notice improvement.

In the process of focusing on the allergy sources in your life, you discover you've been sleeping on a feather pillow. You trade this pillow for one made of a synthetic, nonallergenic material, and suddenly your runny nose and sneezing are gone. You find that you can tolerate the maple tree pollen quite well, and the number of "colds" you have in a year is cut in half.

There is a theory that allergenic conditions can also lower your resistance to cold and flu viruses, making you more susceptible to these infections than perhaps you have to be. Most of the time you have few if any recognizable reactions to the house dust or feathers you confront every day, but when the cold and flu season arrives you have one viral infection after another. If you suspect that something like this is happening to you, you might do well to start scouting around for things in your environment that could be causing your allergic reactions.

Doctors can give you a series of tests to determine whether or not you have any allergies. This can be a moderately expensive and time-consuming process, but it is often a very accurate way of locating the source, or sources, of the problem. Most allergy experts agree that these tests are not 100 percent effective — especially for people who have a high tolerance level but nevertheless do have allergic reactions when their tolerance level is topped. For that reason, using a checklist of allergens is often preferred to the tests.

Allergy clinics offer desensitization programs, which can be helpful for people with allergies beyond their control. But desensitizing is not always successful and can be quite expensive. If at all possible, reduce those common allergens in your life over which you do have some control, and see if that doesn't help you tremendously. You may well discover that this system goes a long way to reduce both your viral infections and your allergic reactions.

Now that you understand something about the diseases and symptoms we've discussed in this chapter, you should have a good set of mental tools for recognizing the complications of cold and flu infections. Remember: Most of the time these complications don't occur. But when they do you now have the knowledge to recognize them quickly — the first step in the healing process. When complications do arise, your doctor's resources can become part of the healing process. But never lose sight of the fact that the most powerful healing powers known to medical science are found in your own body.

Chapter Five

Virus: Villain or Innocent Bystander?

Do you have any choice at all about whether or not you'll get a cold or flu? Yes. But many of us have been taught that the mere presence of a virus means that we'll get that disease. Don't believe it. There are a number of things besides the presence of the virus that lead to the manifestation of disease. If you understand something about what contributes to a virus's ability to cause disease, you begin to have some choice about what you can do to stay healthy.

Although this chapter may seem very theoretical at first, you will soon find that the information presented here provides you with the foundation for understanding the remedies and preventive techniques described in the next chapter.

We live in daily harmony with thousands of different kinds of bacteria and viruses, sharing space, air, water, food, and even our own cells with them. Considering the helpful role that so many of these microbes play in our lives, we might well imagine them resenting the view we sometimes have of them as "enemies." In many cases, life as we know it would be quite impossible without them.

Starting on the smallest scale, there are the mitochondria that live inside each and every cell of our body and resemble plant more than animal life. These beings are in many ways very separate from our cells, and yet without them our cells would not be able to perform the metabolic tasks we require them to do. There are other beings within our cells that have similar relationships with us. As Lewis Thomas, author of *The Lives of a Cell,* expressed it: "My cells are no longer the pure line entities I was raised with; they are ecosystems more complex than Jamaica Bay."

On a slightly larger scale, there are bacteria living in the mucosa of our mouths, stomachs, and intestines that aid in digestion, as well as in our defense against substances that might otherwise harm us. Similarly, streptococci live in our bloodstream, while staphylococci live on our skin surfaces. Adenoviruses live in our nasal passages, and some researchers have even speculated that the existence of these viruses is congenital, since they are found even in the mucosal passages of the newborn.

In a very real sense, each cell within our body is a close relative of each bacterium and virus in the universe. Unlike bacteria, of course, our cells somehow possess the capacity to join with others in the creation of the larger organism we recognize as the human body. Nevertheless, under the close scrutiny of the microscope our cells retain their individual integrity as cells—and indeed show greater kinship with bacteria and viruses than with the larger organism they help to form.

It is therefore easy to understand how biologists and medical scientists have begun to see the entire universe as a community of microorganisms. And within this community the cells that we ordinarily choose to define as our bodies share the universe with more or less equal stature alongside plant cells, bacteria, viruses, and other microorganisms we have not even identified in the laboratory.

In view of this insight into the structure of the universe, we might do well to make peace with our microbial cousins rather than lump them together as a gang of villains out to get us. Science shows that infection does not occur in our bodies because of a simple invasion of foreign organisms. More often it is the result of changes occurring within our bodies, or in our immediate external environment, resulting in viruses or bacteria doing something outside their typical pattern of behavior.

One should realize from the outset that scientists admit they understand but a fraction of everything there is to know about the human body's interrelationships with microorganisms. And yet everything that is known seems to point to the principle that disease is more accidental than intentional in the scheme of the universe. As Lewis Thomas has observed:

> Even in our worst circumstances we have always been a relatively minor interest of the vast microbial world. Pathogenicity is not the rule. Indeed, it occurs so infrequently and involves such a small number of species, considering the huge population of bacteria on the earth, that it has a freakish aspect. Disease usually results from inconclusive negotiations for symbiosis, an overstepping of the line by one side or another, a biologic misinterpretation of borders.

In the study of human disease it is known that the human body's reaction to a "foreign substance" is often the villain causing the symptoms of disease; the foreign substance itself is innocent of any intentional wrongdoing—it has nothing at all to gain by injuring its host. Indeed, there are some microorganisms, brucella being an example, which live for long periods of time in our cells, doing no harm until they are suddenly discovered by our immunological systems; only then does the brucella become active, leading to disease.

Similarly, staphylococci bacteria living on the surface of our skin apparently prevent other bacteria from taking up residence there, and thus they serve a protective function. Ordinarily the staphylococci respect reasonable symbiotic limits whereby they do nothing to harm their host. Yet, on occasion, the presence of staphylococci, combined with our immunological system's response to it, can cause skin problems such as boils.

Why viruses and bacteria can live in an acceptable or even beneficial symbiotic arrangement most of the time, and then suddenly become the source of health problems, is a subject in medical research that still offers more questions than answers. In this field of research one thing is slowly becoming clear: Microorganisms, as a group, are not necessarily alien creatures. They are *essential* to us! In a very real sense, they are as much "us" as our fingers and toes. We couldn't be healthy without them.

Factors causing a disruption in the way we use our microbes, or in the way they use us, are numerous and complex, and much of the work done in this area of inquiry is still inconclusive. But where flu and cold viruses are concerned science does provide us with some important insights, helpful to anyone looking for ways to prevent these infections or shorten the period of illness.

The main areas to be considered here are temperature, nutrition, biorhythms, hormonal levels, stress, concurrent infections, age, and travel.

TEMPERATURE

Temperature can have dramatic effects on the human body and the way our cells interact with viruses. For years there has been debate among medical people about the role of chilling in getting a cold. One medical authority will claim it is a major contributing factor to getting colds or the flu; others say it is totally insignificant. A look at the work of medical researchers on temperature should help us choose between these two stands.

In studies with animals it has been shown that low body temperatures increase the seriousness of viral infections, while raised temperatures tend to reduce their severity. A number of human body functions become sluggish with cold: Circulation to skin surfaces slows; circulation of blood—with all its immunity and healing properties—slows and is ineffective; inflammation—to limit infection from spreading—is reduced. It is also known that many viruses prefer to reproduce in environments which are slightly below the normal temperature of your body. Taken together, then, a low body temperature increases the virus's reproductive capacity but reduces your body's natural abilities to defend itself against infection.

It would be safe to speculate, on the basis of these known medical observations, that chilling can indeed influence your chances of getting a cold or the flu. It must be emphasized, of course, that it is not the chilling itself which causes the infection. Rather, the chilling encourages viruses already present to multiply and, at the same time, set up an environment relatively free of antibodies that might otherwise discourage the virus.

As your body temperature goes up, on the other hand, your immunological system is stimulated and your body produces more interferon. In addition, higher temperatures reduce the capacity of the virus to reproduce. The end result of a higher body temperature is that the reproductive rate of the virus is reduced, while your body produces more antibodies and interferon to render the virus harmless. Figure 6 shows the ranges of your body temperature (taken orally) and what they signify.

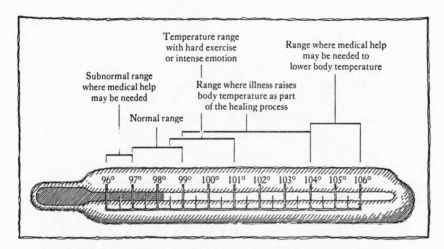

Figure 6: Body Temperature Ranges. This scale shows the range of temperatures you can experience. Most people are surprised to learn that the "normal" range is so wide. Since fever up to 104° can be part of the body's normal healing processes, this must also be viewed as "normal."

NUTRITION

Although it has not been established that the lack of specific vitamins can *cause* a cold or flu, we do know that during even a minor infection, or when you are under stress of any kind, your body has a greater need for certain vitamins than when your life is calm and no infections are present. Thus, what's sufficient at one time in your life may be quite inadequate at another.

It is easy to overlook everyday situations that our bodies respond to as stress. For a great many people, the daily drive to and from work in heavy commute traffic causes enough stress to require extra nutrients for health. That irritated throat or those itchy eyes, produced by smog, may be infection enough to call upon the store of nutrients necessary for restoring peak health.

By studying how our needs for certain nutrients vary, how these needs are increased by a cold, we begin to understand what we might do to maintain optimum health. A person who must commute every day in heavy traffic, and who works in a smoggy area of the city, might discover that by taking certain vitamins and minerals he or she reduces the chance of getting colds and flu.

In this section, I'm going to focus attention on some of the nutritional needs that are particularly important at times of stress and infection. This information, though incomplete at this moment, will serve you to very good advantage when we get into the chapters called "Self-Treatment" and "Creating Health."

No one can dispute the correlations between malnutrition and disease, but there is still much controversy about whether or not a person with a relatively well-balanced diet can increase his or her resistance to disease by taking vitamin supplements or by eating certain foods. It is perhaps an indication of our present worldwide priorities that most of the scientific work done on nutrition and disease has been on severe malnutrition rather than on the improved quality of nutrition. In the words of one researcher (quoted in Frank Fenner and David White's *Medical Virology*):

> It has been repeatedly demonstrated that almost any severe nutritional deficiency will interfere with the production of antibodies and the activity of phagocytes, while the integrity of the skin and mucous membranes is impaired in many types of nutritional deficiency.

Studies have shown that even mild viral infections, in human beings, lead to substantial nitrogen losses. This would indicate very different nutritional needs during illness than during a time when there was no presence of disease. It is also known that the blood levels of vitamins A and C are lowered, even when a person receives a smallpox vaccination—which has the effect of a very minor viral infection.

Vitamin A does a number of important things for one's body, but where a cold or the flu are concerned its beneficial effects on the cells lining the damp mucosal tissue of your nasal passages and throat are of special significance, since it is here that resistance to viral infection begins. Vitamin C has been shown to be essential to health for a great number of reasons—helping your body use iron, aiding the metabolism within the cells, maintaining the strength and elasticity of cell membranes, and affecting the transfer of electrons in your cells. There is, of course, considerable controversy about the usefulness of large doses of vitamin C to prevent colds and the flu, but I've gone into the matter in detail in the chapters which follow.

In view of the findings that blood levels of vitamins A and C are reduced by even minor viral infections, even the most conservative medical person could not disagree that some A and C supplements might help when you have a cold or the flu—and they certainly could do no harm, taken in reasonable amounts. In addition to an increased need for vitamins A and C during an infection, some nutritionists believe that the so-called stress vitamins can help both in the prevention and in the fast recovery from colds and the flu. Stress vitamins include the B-complex group, as well as minerals such as potassium, magnesium, zinc, and calcium.

Remember now, these variations in our nutritional needs occur in a variety of everyday situations ranging from minor stress to small infections. By knowing how minor events can affect our nutritional needs we are alerted to what we might do to prevent small problems from becoming larger ones. Later on, in the chapter called "Creating Health," we'll discuss regular vitamin and mineral supplements to keep you in all-around good health.

BIORHYTHMS

The questions of how and why biological rhythms in nature affect human health have been the subject of a great deal of scientific research. A few years ago a medical writer by the name of Gay Gaer Luce brought this work together in a report published by the U.S. Department of Health, Education, and Welfare and the National Institute of Health. For anyone interested, this information was later published in a more popular form by Ms. Luce in a book called *Body Time.*

The more obvious biological rhythm that affects us is, of course, our body's response to the rotation of the earth on its axis, by which our sleep and waking cycles are organized. Less obvious are the monthly cycles of the moon, a time period that exactly matches the length of the menstrual cycle. Similarly, it has been found that emotions are affected by moon cycles, this being established by the increase in the number of violent acts in jails and mental institutions as well as in the number of cases admitted to hospital emergency rooms during the full moon. In a dramatic study of surgeons in Florida it was established that the incidence of hemorrhages in throat operations was far higher during the second quarter of the moon than at any other time.

More significant for our present purposes, perhaps, is a study that showed the times of the day when people are most susceptible to infection. This information was derived by measuring the gamma globulin levels of the blood at different times of the day—gamma globulin being that portion of the blood which contains antibodies to fight viruses and bacteria. These levels were found to vary as much as 28 percent during the course of the day. Most of the experiments on blood levels were done with animals, but translated to human beings the evidence indicates that our bodies are best at fighting infection at the end of the day. We are most susceptible to infection early in the morning.

Gay Gaer Luce also argues that when we stay up very late at night for a party (or when we fly across the country), we disrupt our sleep patterns. Moreover, we subject ourselves to large groups of people, and thus to potential infection, during those hours when we're normally most open to infection—that is, when our gamma globulin levels are lowest. This may well account for people getting colds, and other infections, more frequently after partying or staying up long hours to study for exams in school.

Some obvious but often overlooked biological rhythms that affect us are the regular seasonal shifts. Early fall and spring bring an increase in the amount of pollen and other natural "pollutants" in the air. For many people, even those who do not think of themselves as hayfever sufferers, the extra stress on the immunological system during these times may leave one open to viral infection.

Winter dryness, caused both by lower humidity and by heating systems that dry the air, tends to dry out nasal passages. When these mucosal areas are dry, their effectiveness for filtering and cleansing the air is greatly reduced, and you become increasingly susceptible to viral infection.

The greater frequency of summer colds in recent years is believed to be due to the increased use of air conditioners. The refrigerated air, in many cases, dries out mucosa-lined passages and also subjects your body to radical shifts from hot to cold and back again as you go in and out of doors. This may cause chilling and a reduction in the effectiveness of your immunological system, as we noted in the discussion of temperature.

By taking careful note of your own rhythms, such as what time of the year you get the most colds or flu, and under what conditions you get them, you may be able to pinpoint the environmental and biological factors that open you to viral infection. Taking these factors into account, an astute observer may be able to make simple, practical changes that will reduce the number of viral infections he or she suffers each year.

HORMONAL LEVELS

Attached to each of your two kidneys are two paired glands that, under certain circumstances, secrete hormonal substances into your bloodstream. One pair of these glands secretes a substance called *cortisol*. It has been established that cortisol reduces your ability to fight infection. It does this by reducing the walling-off effect of inflammation and by decreasing your output of antibodies. Of course, reducing inflammation and decreasing antibody production are not the main purposes of the cortisol secretions. These secretions come in response to potential threats to the organism and prepare you to defend yourself against physical threat. In the latter respect cortisol serves you well indeed — though momentarily reducing resistance to infection.

Ironically, cortisol is secreted in response to events that would seem, at first glance, to call for an increase, not a decrease, in your body's ability to fight infection. For example:

When there is any trauma, emotional or physical
When you are subjected to sudden changes of temperature
When being restrained, or when restraining yourself, against taking action when confronted with a fearful, frustrating, or anger-provoking situation
When you have engaged in physical activities considerably beyond your usual capacities

In all of these cases one should probably try to take conscious steps to avoid contact with people who have colds, the flu, or other infections.

The second paired set of glands above your kidneys secretes *epinephrine* and *norepinephrine*. The epinephrines enter your bloodstream in response to only a few moments of hard physical exercise and increase the metabolic rate of your body as much as 100 percent. With this radical increase in the activity of your circulatory system and within each cell of your body, norepinephrine also has the effect of stimulating the action of certain white blood cells that help you fight infection.

Although there are not, as yet, any clear scientific data to support this opinion, researchers working in athletic medicine have observed that regular physical exercise, such as jogging, bicycling, and swimming, has the effect of stimulating, and therefore strengthening, our natural abilities to resist infection.

Regular exercise is the key word here. It has been clearly established that the amount of norepinephrine secreted during exercise decreases as one's body becomes accustomed to demands being regularly made on it. Since norepinephrine can cause an increase in cortisol secretions (which reduces antibody production), this is a factor well worth considering. Thus, with *regular* exercise, one's body benefits from an increase in metabolic rates, as well as increased activity of white blood cells — without the possibly negative effects of stimulating cortisol secretion.

It is also known that during periods of deep relaxation, especially with conscious relaxation techniques such as meditation, yoga, and even some forms of daydreaming, blood vessels dilate, allowing an increase in the flow of antibodies throughout the system. Although the mechanisms by which this increased flow is accomplished involve nonhormonal as well as hormonal events, the secretion of some hormones, along with the nonsecretion of others, contributes significantly to this process.

STRESS

Although most of us think of stress as something that occurs within our minds in response to difficult life situations, science clearly demonstrates that stress also has profound influences on our bodies. To the physiologist, general terms such as frustration, anxiety, pressure, worry, job tension, conflict, and anger translate into quite specific events taking place inside the body.

During stress, heart and respiration rates change, muscle tension changes, and brain waves change — all seemingly without any conscious effort on our part. Another thing that occurs under stress is the stimulation of the two glands, attached to the kidneys, that produce cortisol. In addition to the secretion of cortisol (which reduces antibody production), your blood flow changes throughout your body. Your body responds to stress in much the same way that it responds to threats of physical attack: During the stressful confrontation, blood flow is directed toward large muscles — such as your back, heart, lungs, arms, legs, and pelvis — and away from organ systems that are not absolutely essential to defending yourself or fleeing.

One of the areas that receives a temporary reduction of blood flow is your digestive system, which includes your mouth and throat. As blood flow slows in those areas, the environment of the mucosal tissues also changes. Have you ever noticed, for example, how your mouth becomes dry when you are nervous or afraid? Stress affects your nasal passages and throat in other ways: For example, it is known that acid levels change. Moist surfaces of mucosal tissue, according to most authorities on the subject, are normally slightly on the acid side. This normal acidity is in a narrow and very specific range, and this ideal range of acidity plays an important part in maintaining a kind of ecological balance within the dampness created by the mucosa. During stress, the ideal range is altered either up or down the acidity scale, sometimes in one direction, sometimes the other. Any such alteration can affect normal resistance and even induce a higher reproductive rate on the part of viruses. Temperature also changes under stress. Temperature is maintained by blood flow and we know that blood flow is reduced in the outer skin layers of the mouth during stress.

Taken together, then, stress creates some major changes in the nasal passages and mouth: reduced antibody production, reduced blood flow, reduced moisture, and reduced acid level. How can these changes affect your health? Anyone who has studied ecology knows that as you change, let's say, the heat of the water in a small pond, the balance of life forms living in that water will change. Some organisms will reproduce more rapidly than normal while others will reproduce less rapidly. Food chains will change, and as a result some organisms will die of starvation.

This sequence of events is a direct parallel to what happens in your mouth during times of stress. Viruses or bacteria that lived there in peaceful symbiosis yesterday begin reproducing at different rates, resulting in changes that encourage overreproduction of viruses which would otherwise be either harmless or actually helpful. (It is known that our bodies learn to tolerate certain viruses and bacteria. Such microbes live in our bodies in perfect harmony, and even stake out their territory so that viruses and bacteria which our bodies can't immediately tolerate are prevented from taking hold.)

The lesson we learn from this is that during times of stress you should make an effort to avoid people with infection, do everything you can to resolve the sources of conflict in your life, and learn relaxation techniques to develop more conscious control of your inner environments. These are techniques we discuss in greater detail in the chapters that follow.

CONCURRENT INFECTIONS

Infection itself is a form of stress and as such can open you to other infections. By reducing an area of stress in your life, and by giving more energy over to your body's self-healing mechanisms, the small infection can be stopped and fear of more serious infection eliminated.

On the lowest end of the disease scale, you should recognize that a minor infection such as a slight case of diarrhea, or a skin infection such as a boil, or even an infected cut in your finger, can lower your resistance to cold or flu viruses. Extra care in treating the minor infection — and of course in avoiding other people with colds or flu — can be a major preventive measure during these times.

AGE

How does age relate to one's resistance to colds and flu? Let's start at the higher end of the scale, old age, which is often associated in the public mind with poor health. In recent years research has demonstrated that old age need not be synonymous with poor health. As one physician explained to me recently, a person's physical well-being reflects one's lifelong habits. If for sixty-five years that person has lived a sedentary, neglectful life, from a health standpoint, this pattern will be reflected in his or her body. On the other hand, if one has lived a physically active live, with good nutrition and reasonable amounts of personal satisfaction, it is this pattern that will be reflected in his or her body and general state of well-being. The old adage that you get the face you deserve when you're forty might well be applied to one's health, too!

The stereotype of the older person who sits around all day long, living only for the next brief visit from the grandchildren, is quickly being dispelled by thousands of retirement-age people starting new careers for themselves, taking up athletic activities, even returning to school to prepare for new professions. But, of course, the stereotypes do persist, and one should consider how an extremely sedentary existence might affect one's health. The human body functions best with a certain amount of vigorous physical activity. As we've noted in the preceding pages, higher metabolic rates and increased production of antibodies, both of which result from regular exercise, build a natural resistance to disease.

On the other hand, a person who is breathing very shallowly—which is not uncommon in people who avoid hard physical exercise, as far too many older people do—barely keeps the respiratory system toned. Minor viral infections can, in such persons, invite more serious bacterial complications, typically the pneumonias, which can move down into the lungs. Basically, this is why many doctors are quick to prescribe antibiotics for older patients who are having difficulty shaking a cold.

On the opposite end of the age scale, we have the problem of youth. Although the youthful, active person is more capable of overcoming infection in most cases, he or she often does not possess the antibodies an older person might. This difference is exemplified by the "childhood diseases": measles, mumps, chickenpox, and the like (all viral infections). Most people develop antibodies before they reach high school age. Just as the speech centers of the infant's brain are learning to recognize and form words, so the infant's immunological system is learning to recognize viruses and bacteria and form antibodies against them.

Although the protection one receives from the production of antibodies against the common cold is not long-lasting—a year or so at the most—there is longer protection by acquired immunity from many forms of influenza. Thus, in influenza epidemics, which tend to go in twenty to thirty year cycles, it is often the younger, rather than the older, person who has the highest incidence of infection or suffers the most. The reason is that the older person has developed antibodies against that particular flu virus as a result of previous infection, say up to twenty years before. This type of immunity is not always 100 percent effective, but even when it's not, it often means that the older person will have a less severe case of the flu than the younger person.

The infant, of course, inherits some immunities from its mother, and these immunities generally remain effective throughout the first months of the child's life, especially with the infant of a nursing mother. Thereafter, for many children, those first four or five years can seem like one continuous cold.

Of course, coldlike symptoms can have many sources, ranging from allergies to nutritional deficiencies. If you have a child with a constantly runny nose, or a cough, you should ask your doctor to advise you. Most pediatricians will be glad to provide you with checklists to help you locate allergenic substances or even identify nutritional deficiencies through a painless process of trial and error. As the infant's body is subjected to numerous viruses, he or she develops symptoms, actually gets the disease, and in the process develops antibodies to prevent or reduce the severity of future infection. Just as experience in the world challenges the infant to crawl, then walk, and finally run, so the immunological system must develop experience in producing antibodies against viral and bacterial infection.

Most physicians agree that the symptoms of the common cold and flu should be watched in infants—partly because young children can be quite vulnerable to a variety of diseases that begin with respiratory symptoms (measles, for example), but also because the infant is usually unable to cough or blow its nose in order to clear the air passages. The inability to clear mucus from the throat and nose, as adults can do, also makes the infant more vulnerable where the complications of colds and flu are concerned.

TRAVEL

It has been observed that in small, isolated communities the common cold and flu are almost nonexistent. Apparently the small, stable population maintains an immunity against the limited number of viruses in its environment. If a person comes into that community from the outside, however, and brings a new batch of viruses along, infection will spread through that community until antibodies have formed against it.

Living in a modern city or suburb, most of us are subjected each day to new viruses brought into our communities by people traveling to and from all points on the globe. Similarly, when traveling to other communities, we find ourselves subjected to viruses that are unknown to our bodies and against which we have not yet formed any antibodies.

The speed at which we travel these days, and the amount of travel being done both by vacationers and by business people, pretty well guarantees a thorough mixing of the viral stew. A virus originating on one coast of our country turns up on the other in a matter of days. A virus discovered in Europe finds its way to our shores in a matter of weeks. Compared to people living in isolated rural communities, the immunological system of the contemporary city or suburb dweller is busy indeed!

So people traveling from one community to another not only become subjected to viruses new to them but also bring new viruses into the places they visit. In any case, travel becomes a potential cause of colds and flu from at least two angles.

A BACKWARD GLANCE

I trust by now the point is clear that there are many factors beyond the simple existence of a virus that can give rise to a cold or the flu. Among them are the things we've discussed here — temperature, nutrition, biorhythms, hormonal levels, stress, concurrent infections, age, and travel.

So where are we at this point in developing our program for self-treatment? We started by examining what happens inside us when we get a cold or flu. Next we learned how to recognize potential complications of colds and flu. And now we've just finished the consideration of several factors that can contribute to a person's getting a cold or flu. Having done all that, we now have the information we need to consider the whole matter of self-treatment, the subject of the next chapter.

References

Lewis Thomas, M.D.: *The Lives of a Cell* (New York: Viking Press, 1974).
Frank Fenner and David White: *Medical Virology* (New York: Academic Press, 1976).
Gay Gaer Luce: *Biological Rhythms in Psychiatry and Medicine* (Washington: Public Health Service, 1970).
Gay Gaer Luce: *Body Time* (New York: Pantheon Books, 1971).
Jan Praetorius Clausen: "Effect of Physical Training on Cardiovascular Adjustments to Exercise in Man," *Physiological Reviews* (October 1977).
Richie R. Ward: *The Living Clocks* (New York: Knopf, 1971).

Chapter Six

Self-Treatment

In this chapter we'll put to practical use all the theoretical infor-mation presented thus far in the book. Presented here are a number of alternatives to over-the-counter or prescription drugs commonly offered by doctors. These include recipes and descriptions for remedies that you can use to aid your own body's natural healing processes. Much more than a potpourri, this chapter gives you clear-cut plans for putting together treatment programs to min-imize your discomfort and speed your recovery the next time you have a cold or flu.

Whenever you do get a cold or flu, you want comfort and relief right away. The temptation, for many people, is to run to the drug-store and buy the cold pills they saw advertised on television the night before. Resist that temptation. It's likely that past experience has already proved these medications don't help you anyway. If they had helped you, you probably wouldn't be reading this book right now. Besides, many over-the-counter cold remedies cause more problems than they solve, working against your self-healing processes rather than cooperating with them. But that's a subject we'll discuss in the chapter on drugs, which follows this one.

In this chapter, we look first at how to head off a cold or flu in the early stages and then go into what you can do if you've got one. After that, I describe what might loosely be called "remedies." These are organized in four basic categories: grandma remedies, nutrition, emotions, and exercise.

As you're reading through this chapter for the first time, be thinking about what I believe to be the universal principle of healing: The quickest relief you'll get is that which you create for yourself by making adjustments in your daily life. These adjustments, aimed at providing your body with the best advantages for healing, are the basis of the program I describe in this chapter. The key word in this program is "comfort." Comfort is a universal medicine that we vastly underrate. It is the fuel of that powerful self-healing machinery we all possess.

HOW EARLY TREATMENT CAN HELP YOU

Depending upon whether it's a cold or the flu, you may be able to start your treatment program early and rid yourself of the virus before you have any significant discomfort. Remember, colds creep up on you gradually. Flu, on the other hand, tends to come on suddenly, giving little or no opportunity to take action to heal it early on in the game. So for now let's put the flu aside and concentrate on the common cold.

Most people, once they've learned to do so, can recognize the earliest symptoms of a cold and take action against further infection right away. The earliest symptoms are different for different people, and probably vary according to the specific virus involved, but in general they are:

> A slight throat tickle
> A feeling of being slightly out of sorts: mildly distracted, tense, physically uncoordinated
> Nose or throat feels tight or perhaps dry
> Appetite doesn't seem normal

Think back over the last time you had a cold and try to recall if you noticed any of these symptoms a day or so before you got a runny nose or sore throat. You may not have considered them important at the time, or perhaps you didn't associate them with a cold.

The next time you notice these early symptoms, pay attention to them. Look upon them as signals from your body to slow down a little, to give yourself a bit more comfort that day. How do you do that? Here's a list of suggestions:

> Reduce your work load. For most people this can be accomplished by not taking on anything extra that day, no matter how small that extra task may seem.
> Treat yourself to extra fluids, preferably fruit juices that contain nutrients to help your body build antibodies.

Instead of anticipating other people's needs, wait until they make their needs clearly known to you. This will reduce tension considerably once you learn to do it.

Several times during the day, pause and take a few moments to daydream about something you particularly enjoy doing. Simply indulge these mental wanderings for a moment or two, and then let them go.

Slow your walking pace whenever you move about. Let your shoulders be loose, and let your jaw be slack as you move. Be as languorous as you can without feeling silly about it. The changes need be only subtle ones to be beneficial.

Eat a light but enjoyable meal that evening, and retire early.

These small changes may well be all that is necessary to give your body the extra energy it needs to heal the cold. What you're doing here, in essence, is rechanneling energy from daily routines and letting it be used by your body's self-healing mechanisms. But remember, it's important to continue these energy-conserving tech-

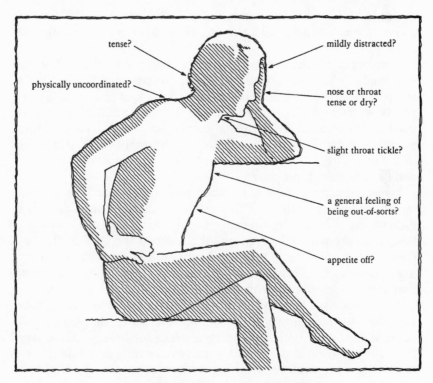

Figure 7: The Earliest Symptoms of Cold and Flu.

niques as long as a day or two after all of your symptoms have disappeared. By doing so you give your body a chance to heal itself completely.

Relaxation of shoulder and jaw muscles, in particular, allows blood flow to increase in your nose and throat areas, and in some people it also allows moisture levels in those sites to return to normal. By relaxing more, by reducing stress, by going into the mental state required to daydream (a meditative state), you establish hormonal levels where antibody production is maximized. In a relaxed state your immunity system is working far better than it does when you are under physical and emotional stress. By creating comfort in these ways, you literally create a healing state in your body, which in most cases will prevent your early cold from getting any worse.

WHAT IF IT JUST GETS WORSE?

But let's say you don't notice the early signals of a cold. Or you wake up one morning with the flu. What's the basic healing program to follow?

Comfort is still the key word. With a cough, a sore throat, fever, and headache, creating comfort is going to require a different set of techniques than you followed for the early stages of a cold. Before you were trying to lighten your load, but now you feel as though you have to break away completely from your usual routines. However, the principle that served you in the early stage still holds true here: Create comfort in your life; channel energy to your body's self-healing processes.

What happens to most of us when we get a cold or flu is that we try to push through the first day or two of discomfort as though it didn't exist. We can be sneezing and hacking but still doing our best to ignore what's happening. We pretend the cold or flu isn't there or that it will disappear any moment. The time we spend trying to ignore our symptoms can actually be prolonging the period that the viruses will be with us.

The sooner you are able to withdraw from your usual routine, and slow yourself down to a comfortable pace, the sooner you provide your body with the energy it needs for healing. Give your body the medicine of comfort as soon as you can. The tendency, for most of us, is to continue working until we're too uncomfortable to do so. Not until then do we feel justified in taking time off. In terms of health, in terms of keeping the cold or flu manageable, in terms of minimizing complications, and potentially reducing the total number of days sick, it makes much better sense to start your healing program before you're too uncomfortable to do anything else.

What I'm suggesting is that you start the healing program while you can still enjoy the comfort of a day off. Go home and be as lazy as you wish. Take warm baths. Drink lots of your favorite fruit juices. Let yourself daydream about a special vacation trip. Lie around and read, or watch television, or listen to the radio. Whenever you have choices to make that day make them on the basis of whether they will add to your comfort.

If you feel guilty about leaving your work behind so that you can enjoy yourself in this way, remind yourself that this day of comfort is being put to productive use. It is a day to turn over your energies to the healing mechanisms of your body. And in the long run, your treatment program may well be responsible for reducing the total number of days you are sick.

In our work together, Dr. Mike Samuels and I have frequently discussed how minor illnesses, such as colds and flu, can often be viewed as signals to change something to improve one's life. In other words, sometimes disease is a positive occurrence in your life. Many doctors share this opinion, especially as it applies to colds. There is a theory that colds work as safety valves to slow you down before you get a more serious disease.

Try looking upon colds in this way: not as diseases that have suddenly come out of nowhere to victimize you, but as part of your body's self-healing dynamic. Let the cold be; do what it's telling you to do. Slow down. Take the pressure off yourself. Enjoy a day or two of leisure. Reflect on how to make your life more enjoyable from moment to moment.

During the time you're at home providing your body with the medicine of comfort, you may wish to try some of the remedies I describe in this chapter. As you read through them, notice how they are all aimed at providing comfort. I recommend them here because they aid the healing processes of your body.

I believe that drugs can be helpful at certain times in our lives, but my own use of them is based on a very moderate principle: Use them only when they can help, rather than hinder, the normal healing processes. I'll elaborate on this point later on in the chapter on drugs.

WHEN IT'S TIME FOR GRANDMA'S HELP

We've talked about programs for heading off a cold at its first symptoms, and what to do when things have gotten bad enough for a day off. But let's say that regardless of what you do the cold or flu gets worse and it has become necessary to stay at home a number of days and nurse yourself through. Is this the time to bring out the cold pills? I still say no. Keep focused on the principle that comfort is the best medicine, even though that comfort is going to be more difficult to achieve now than it was in the very first days of your cold or flu.

Begin this step of the treatment program by addressing yourself to any of those nagging anxieties you may have about your symptoms. Read through the chapter called "When Is a Cold Not?" to dispel your concern and make a decision about how you're going to proceed. Remember, putting your mind at ease, reducing your anxieties by understanding your symptoms, is an important *comfort*. Here's an example of how your knowledge directly benefits your general health.

In the following pages I describe a number of cold and flu remedies in a more or less random order. The program at this point is to go through the remedies and choose the ones that most appeal to you. Which ones look like they would bring you the most comfort? Make your choices on that basis, and don't hesitate to use all of them at once, if that appeals to you, or to establish your own treatment plan built around a few.

The remedies described here are not the only ones that are effective in the kind of cold and flu treatment programs we're discussing. These just happen to be some I know about that fit the basic principle of comfort as medicine and also bring some degree of relief from symptoms. You may know of other remedies that work effectively for you. By all means, if they work for you then integrate them into your own treatment program.

GRANDMA'S COMFORTS

Nearly everyone has a grandmother or great-grandmother who has passed along her own "cure" for the common cold. A few of these, which I've collected from various sources over the years, seem worthy of repeating here.

Cozying Up

Take a very hot bath, as hot as you can stand, and then snuggle up in a nice warm bed. Remain there the whole day and through that night, even if doing so means you're neglecting your family. Read a good book or write letters to special friends who are far away. Drink lots of fluids.

In addition to the warm bath and bed, there were teas and potions one took to relieve aches, pains, a cough, or a stuffy nose. For a scratchy or sore throat, there was:

Hot Lemon Tea

Add two whole lemons to a pot of boiling water. Let steep for ten minutes. Drink with a tablespoon of honey to the cup.

For a scratchy throat with nasal or sinus congestion there was:

Hot Ginger Milk

Heat, but do not boil, a pan of milk. To this add two or three slices of fresh ginger. If fresh isn't available, use ¼ to ¾ teaspoon of ground ginger from the supermarket. Serve hot with honey to taste.

A variation of these remedies was:

Vinegar and Honey

Mix equal parts (1 tablespoon each) of apple cider vinegar and honey in hot water to relieve nasal congestion and aches. Can also be used to gargle.

Some cures were potent indeed:

Herbs

Herbalists today base most of their remedies on age-old recipes handed down from one generation to another. Teas such as comfrey, chamomile, rose hips, and peppermint are used by many people to relieve symptoms of the common cold and flu. Teas of cayenne (red pepper) are said to be excellent for relieving a cough.

Cod Liver Oil and Garlic

A remedy for a cold or flu, which most of us probably prefer to forget, is that dose of cod liver oil two or three times a day. Or how about swallowing three or four mashed cloves of garlic?

This one's a bit easier to take:

For Sniffles and Stuffy Nose

Drink a half teaspoon of salt and the same of soda in warm water, four or five times a day.

For problems of digestion, which are often associated with colds and flu, there were the following specific remedies:

For Diarrhea

Make as a tea equal parts of raspberry leaves, peppermint, and comfrey.

Or: Carob and honey in water only, since milk can aggravate the problem. Some vanilla can be added for flavor.

Or: A half teaspoon of nutmeg, made as a tea or swallowed with a bit of honey if you wish, taken several times a day.

For Indigestion

Make teas of chamomile, dandelion, or peppermint. Papaya teas are good when you can get them.

By far the most appetizing traditional recipe that I've come across is one Mike Samuels got from his wife, who got it from her grandmother. We included it in *The Well Body Book* for relief of constipation. Because it is both an effective and an enjoyable recipe, I repeat it here:

Grandmother Pelton's Chocolate-Molasses Cookies

1 cup brown sugar	3 egg yolks, beaten
1 cup equal parts butter and vegetable shortening	3 squares bitter chocolate, melted
1 pint molasses	½ cup hot water, with 1 teaspoon baking soda
1 teaspoon cinnamon	3½ cups pastry flour (or enough to make soft dough)
1 teaspoon ground cloves	

Use a heaping tablespoon of batter for each cookie, dropping them onto a greased cookie sheet. Bake 12 to 15 minutes at 350°. Yield: about 4 dozen large cookies.

WHY OLD REMEDIES WORK

Many traditional remedies have survived from generation to generation for the simple reason that they work. Sometimes the remedies are effective because, like the doctor prescribing cold pills, one feels better doing something, rather than sulking around waiting for nature to take its course. But sometimes there is a physiological basis for the traditional remedies, and I've found it intriguing to attempt to trace what some of these might be.

The physiological basis for the first remedy mentioned here, "Cozying Up," is in some ways the most obvious. The main ingredient here is warmth, a subject we investigated in our discussion of temperature. We know that heat increases the body's production of natural substances to reduce the viruses' ability to reproduce. Moreover, it speeds up the body's metabolic rate, creating an active rather than a sluggish system, for cleansing away dead cells and creating new cells to replace those damaged by the viruses. And by raising your body temperature you make a less inviting environment for the viruses. In addition, the warmth relaxes you. This absence of stress, we know, is particularly therapeutic — not only because it opens tiny capillaries throughout your body, thus increasing the flow of blood to areas of infection, but also because it keeps down your production of the hormone cortisol, which can reduce antibody production.

Similarly, relaxation is important in that part of the remedy which suggests writing letters to friends who are far away. During such an activity you can daydream about pleasurable times you spent with those friends in the past, and this open, relaxed mental state, similar to some meditative states, has a definite beneficial healing effect.

Finally, drinking plenty of liquids is important in maintaining a healthy fluid level in your body. With your body temperature raised you use up a lot more moisture than usual, and it is essential to maintain that fluid level at all times. The hot teas, such as lemon, ginger, and the vinegar and honey recipes, probably help relieve scratchy or sore throat in two ways: First, they stimulate blood flow to the mucosal tissue of your throat; and second, they may help change the alkaline environment of your throat to a healthier acid level. Of course, lemon, ginger, and vinegar also have the effect of relieving congestion, probably by stimulating those cells in the mucosal tissue of both nasal passage and throat that produce fluids to thin thickened mucus.

It is doubtful whether there's much vitamin C left in grandma's lemons after dropping them in boiling hot water, but perhaps some of the less well known citrus substances do live through this hot bath. More likely, it is the acid content of the lemons or the vinegar in these two recipes that provides the most benefits by helping to reestablish, at least temporarily, the acid levels that maintain your throat in a healthy state.

That old standby, cod liver oil, is clearly beneficial since it is a fact that your body uses many times more vitamin A when you have an infection, and cod liver oil is loaded with that vitamin. It also contains vitamin D, and since most colds occur in the winter, when most of us are indoors—out of the sun, which is our main source of this vitamin—that couldn't hurt either. As for the mashed garlic, vitamins A, B, C, D, and E are richly provided there, as are minerals such as potassium, some calcium, and magnesium. All of these are known to be used in great quantity by your body whenever you have an infection. For those who prefer the cold symptoms over the taste of these potions, there are capsulized forms available at some drugstores and certainly at most health food stores.

The effective ingredients of herbs and teas such as comfrey and chamomile are hard to trace. There's little known about their active ingredients though there are a great many people who find them soothing and "medicinally beneficial." Perhaps like aspirin their active ingredients will remain forever elusive to the exacting eye of the medical scientist.

Salt and soda have the power to reduce the amount of fluids secreted from areas that are inflamed as a result of infection. During most infections your body loses sodium, so replacing it can, at least temporarily, make the capillaries less sievelike, slowing down the fluids emptying into the infected areas.

Papaya, which is recommended for upset stomachs, is known to contain enzymes that aid the digestive processes, especially where the normal breaking down of fat is concerned. The breakdown of fat is also important for the absorption of vitamins A, D, E, and K, which you need in great abundance when you have an infection. And, finally, the cookie recipe contains abundances of molasses and chocolate, which taken in combination can have a gentle laxative effect.

NUTRITION

Nowhere in the field of medical education is there a greater lack than in nutrition. Except for special diets designed for ulcer patients, diabetics, and the like, medical textbooks are all but devoid of information pertaining to the stuff we all live by: food.

Does this mean that no serious research has been done on food? No. On the contrary, a good deal of work has been carried out. Why it isn't more integrated with the standard medical education programs is probably a matter of priorities. Most doctors, we must remember, spend a good part of their medical education working with patients in hospitals who have serious diseases — diseases that often require immediate, decisive action, such as surgery or drug therapy. Nutritional changes require time and patience, ingredients that neither the acutely ill nor their physicians can afford.

Because they lack any substantial background in nutrition, many physicians perhaps jump to the conclusion that it has no validity: "They didn't include it in my medical education, so it can't be very important." This state of affairs is beginning to change. If the institutions of learning fail to incorporate a study of nutrition into their programs, some doctors are going out on their own to learn about it. It is one of those peculiarities of history that physicians have neglected the relationship between good nutrition and health. The medical textbooks accept the relationship between extreme malnutrition and disease but one must look outside those treatises for research which goes beyond that.

Vitamin C: My Contribution to the Controversy

In Linus Pauling's *Vitamin C, the Common Cold and the Flu,* there is a short history of the medical community's resistance to accepting vitamin C for the prevention and treatment of scurvy. Literally thousands of sailors died of scurvy in the great sea voyages from the 1400s up to the latter half of the nineteenth century. All these deaths occurred in spite of the fact that the cure and prevention of scurvy had been demonstrated as far back as 1536 when the French explorer Jacques Cartier was shown by a North American Indian how to make a tea rich in vitamin C from the leaves and bark of the arborvitae tree, which saved the lives of his crew.

In 1747, a Scottish physician by the name of James Lind documented his work with patients who had scurvy but got well after eating citrus fruits. That and other studies on the treatment of scurvy were published in his *Treatise on Scurvy* in 1753. And yet, in spite of Dr. Lind's carefully documented work, the theory remained controversial in the medical community for nearly fifty years. In 1795 the British Admiralty finally accepted Lind's findings and thereafter required a daily ration of limes for every sailor in the Royal Navy. Seventy years later a similar acceptance was expressed in the private sector when the British Board of Trade established lime rations for the merchant marines.

In recent years, Linus Pauling's work on vitamin C to prevent respiratory illnesses might or might not be compared to the work of Dr. Lind. In studying the research literature, I find nearly as many supporters as I find detractors for Pauling's theories. I suppose we will all have to wait another seventy to a hundred years to find out what's going to happen. In the meantime, thousands of people across the nation religiously take their 1 to 10 grams of vitamin C every day, convinced, or not convinced, by their experiences, or Dr. Pauling, or both, that it really does some good. (Remember that 1000 milligrams equals 1 gram; that's up to 10,000 milligrams a day.) Everyone I know who does this swears that they have fewer colds and flu, and when they do get upper respiratory illnesses the symptoms are mild.

I take up to 3 grams of vitamin C each day during the winter cold season — doubling that if I feel a cold coming on. On a few occasions, after having gotten a cold, I've noticed a dramatic reduction in my symptoms the day after taking 6 to 8 grams.

It is a medical fact that without vitamin C our bodies become less and less capable of self-healing, more and more susceptible to disease, and increasingly incapable of handling stress. In fact, humans will eventually die if deprived of vitamin C entirely. Since our bodies produce no vitamin C on their own — unlike many other animals — we are wholly dependent on food for this essential health-giving vitamin. The debate is not centered on the fact that we need it but on the quantity we need, and whether or not *any* quantity has a significant effect on infections such as cold or flu.

Studies published in the British medical journal *The Lancet,* in the 24 June 1972 issue, told about research demonstrating that large quantities of vitamin C tended to reduce the severity of colds. Similar findings were published in the *Canadian Medical Association Journal* for September 1972, this time based on scientific research carried out by a physician who had earlier attacked Pauling's theories. Both of these were dependable scientific studies, carried out by unquestionably competent researchers.

As to the exact doses where vitamin C becomes effective, no one is sure, although there is plenty to indicate that each person's body chemistry is highly individualized and that wide variations in body chemistry mean that what's enough for one person is a deprivation for others. Numerous studies cited by Dr. Roger J. Williams in his *Nutrition Against Disease* told how animals of the same age, species, environment, and general diet had vitamin A and C needs that varied as much as forty times from one animal to another.

As to why vitamin C does what it does, no one seems to be exactly sure. The truth is, it does many things. Some are of the opinion that vitamin C strengthens the membrane of each cell. Perhaps making it less inviting to viral attachment or penetration. Others have shown how vitamin C aids the body in making proper use of other necessary nutrients, iron among them; this is an important factor that accounts for this vitamin's ability to help us resist infection.

The most interesting statement made about vitamin C is one I found in a book called *Natural Healing* by Mark Bricklin. Research at Stanford University by Dr. Carlton E. Schwendt and Patricia Schwendt, both biochemists, demonstrated that vitamin C apparently acts inside the cells in a manner similar to that of interferon.

I think we're living at one of those points in history when even though the evidence appears to be stacking up in favor of vitamin C, full acceptance by the medical community is yet to come. It is, I believe, important to seek the truth in this matter not only to settle the controversy Pauling stirred up but also because in the process we will undoubtedly learn more about our own bodies' miraculous self-healing capacities.

In the final analysis, it is the public's own firsthand experience with vitamin C and respiratory infection that will settle the controversy once and for all. In the meantime, scientists will continue their studies and debates, keeping the fire going long enough for the rest of us to find out for ourselves what works and what doesn't.

Does Vitamin C Cause Side Effects?

Since the popularization of large doses of vitamin C for preventing the common cold and flu, many rumors have circulated concerning its potential side effects. The side effects supposedly attributable to megadoses of this vitamin include diarrhea, kidney stones, ulcers, and depletion of vitamin B12. Linus Pauling, in his book *Vitamin C, the Common Cold and the Flu,* has done exhaustive research on all these claims and has proved, for the most part, that they are unfounded.

Diarrhea can, he admits, be caused, in some people, by taking large doses of vitamin C—especially when they have just begun taking those large doses. In most cases, however, he found that people adjusted to the high doses in a matter of days, even when doses were as high as 40 grams a day. In a few cases, he found that if one changed the brand of vitamin C one was using the discomforts of diarrhea or gas were reduced or stopped altogether.

Flavoring additives or coloring, added to some vitamin C tablets, can contribute to problems with diarrhea or gas with some people, Dr. Pauling points out. He also notes that some people can apparently handle pure crystalline ascorbic acid, sodium ascorbic, or a mixture of these, better than they can handle more commonly available vitamin C tablets.

On the subject of vitamin C and the formation of kidney stones, Dr. Pauling answers that "not a single case has been reported in the medical literature of a person who formed kidney stones because of a large intake of vitamin C." He further observes that among those people who do form kidney stones (for reasons not in any way associated with the intake of vitamin C), there are two classes. One class of stones forms in alkaline urine, the other in acidic urine. According to Dr. Pauling, many physicians treat alkaline-formed kidney stones by acidifying the urine with a gram or more of vitamin C. On the other hand, people who tend to form kidney stones when their urine becomes acidic are advised to take their vitamin C as sodium ascorbate, or to take it with an alkalizer to maintain their urine on the alkaline side.

In answer to the question of whether or not vitamin C can cause ulcers, Dr. Pauling states:

"Some people have asked me if ascorbic acid, by acting as an acid, might not cause stomach ulcers. In fact, the gastric juice in the stomach contains a strong acid, and ascorbic acid, which is a weak acid, does not increase its acidity. Aspirin tablets and potassium chloride tablets can erode the wall of the stomach and cause ulcers. Vitamin C keeps them [ulcers] from forming and helps to heal them."

In answer to some medical critics who claimed that megadoses of vitamin C could cause the depletion of vitamin B12 in our bodies, Dr. Pauling showed that the researchers who originally made this claim reran their experiments and discovered their findings in error. In summary, Dr. Pauling states that "they were led to draw an incorrect conclusion by having used a poor method of chemical analysis for vitamin B12."

Another factor worth consideration when you are taking large doses of vitamin C is what some people have called the "rebound effect." In his research, Dr. Pauling shows that if you are taking large doses of vitamin C and you suddenly decrease your intake of that vitamin, the amount of usable vitamin C in your blood stream *could* fall below the level necessary for fighting infection. He states, however, that the "rebound effect probably is not very important for most people." Still, if you are taking large doses of vitamin C, and you are considering reducing that dosage, it is probably wise to do so gradually, and over a period of a week or two.

Beyond Vitamin C

Whenever you have an infection—and colds or the flu are no exceptions—your body has different nutritional needs than when you are well. One of our most famous nutritionists, Adelle Davis, recommended (in *Let's Get Well*) what she called her "antistress formula" for people with illnesses such as the upper respiratory diseases. I believe that the antistress formula does, in fact, insure that your body will be getting everything it needs to keep its natural healing capacities working at their best.

Antistress Formula

Take with every meal, and before going to sleep, 500 milligrams or more of vitamin C, 100 milligrams of pantothenic acid, and at least 2 milligrams each of vitamin B2 and B6. Take these supplements with fortified milk so that you are sure to get enough protein. Every day eat fresh or desiccated liver (which you can get at a health food store); a cooked green leafy vegetable; wheat germ; and vitamins A, D, and E.

Much of this advice conforms to what we already know about the nutritional changes that occur in our bodies when we have an infection. For example, we have already discussed the need for increased vitamin A and C. According to Adelle Davis, her opinion about the need for pantothenic acid and B6 is based on evidence that animals "even mildly deficient in pantothenic acid or B6 show an immediate marked reduction in antibodies, complement, and white blood cells." Science shows that protein is used in great abundance by the body to produce antibodies and white blood cells to fight infection; being certain you get enough protein when you have an infection provides your body with the building nutrients it needs. Moreover, we know that in order to absorb vitamin C adequately we must get enough calcium in our diets and to use calcium properly we must have enough vitamin D. Thus the D vitamin and the calcium-rich milk are needed.

Lost Vitamins

Many nutritionists say that we lack vitamin A in our diets, in part because nitrites, used as preservatives in meats such as ham, cold cuts, frankfurters, salami, and many other sausages, prevent our bodies from being able to use this important vitamin. Other substances antagonistic to vitamin A are benzoate of soda, used as a preservative in a variety of foods, and citral, used as a lemonlike flavoring in desserts and drinks. Moreover, the B vitamins and vitamin C are known to be destroyed, or made less effective in our bodies, by alcohol and caffeine-containing beverages.

On Orange Juice

While we're on the subject of how vitamins are affected by substances mixed with our foods, or by food preparation, we should discuss orange juice as a source of vitamin C. Many people believe that because they drink a big glass of "O.J." for breakfast they are getting enough vitamin C in their diets. If the juice is freshly squeezed, they are getting something like 150 milligrams of C (about three times the adult minimum daily requirement). If you are drinking canned orange drinks, however, you may be getting no vitamin C at all!

Vitamin C is not very stable: It is destroyed by boiling as well as by freezing. Frozen orange juices vary greatly as to how they're made — some are quick-frozen, some are dehydrated first and then quick-frozen, and so on. So the amount of C will vary from brand to brand. But all canned or frozen orange juices provide fewer nutrients than good quality fresh juice. I'll let you be the judge of how much vitamin C you're getting from your favorite canned or frozen brand.

On Yogurt

Although not a great deal is known about all the mechanisms that make it effective, a bacterium present in some yogurt, *Lactobacillus acidophilus,* helps maintain the normal, helpful bacterial population in your digestive system. Some nutritionists say that taking acidophilus tablets, or eating large amounts of a good quality yogurt, helps your body fight infection. In part, this has to do with your stomach's role in destroying bacteria and viruses trapped in the mucosal blanket that empties into it. Try eating yogurt or acidophilus tablets when you have diarrhea or when you are taking antibiotics. The lactobacillus helps your body restore normal intestinal flora destroyed by these conditions.

When you buy yogurt in the supermarket be sure to read the label. Many of the flavored yogurts, in particular, are made from gelatin, sugar, milk fat thickeners, sugar, and artificial flavoring, with only enough yogurt culture added to legally call it that. In short, they are a sort of milk pudding with artificial flavorings and binders added. Try health food stores if you have any trouble getting a true acidophilus yogurt in your local stores.

On Milk

From time to time nutritionists appear on the scene who tell us that milk may be either a contributing factor or a cause of respiratory diseases. Such a person is N. W. Walker, president of Norwalk Laboratory of Nutritional Chemistry and Scientific Research. In one of his books, *Diet and Salad,* he stated: "Milk is the most mucus forming food in the human dietary, and from infancy to senility it is the most insidious cause of colds, flu, bronchial troubles, asthma, hay fever, pneumonia, tuberculosis and sinus trouble, according to our experience." Although he offers no scientific basis for his views, Walker defends his position by saying: "There is not a member of the animal kingdom which uses milk as food after it has been weaned. It remains for man to develop such stupidity and to overlook the use of milk as the cause of so many of his ailments."

Personally, I'm not convinced that milk causes colds or flu but I do find it less appetizing when I have an upper respiratory illness. I also have several friends and acquaintances who report that they feel less congested when they restrict or completely cut out milk during the healing period of a cold or flu. The practice may be worth trying the next time you have a cold or flu. You may well enjoy some benefits by substituting fruit juices, teas, or just plain water for milk. We do know that milk is an excellent medium for growing microorganisms, and for that reason many doctors recommend cutting it out when you have diarrhea or intestinal flu. Perhaps the same mechanism is at work in your mouth and throat when you drink milk with a cold.

On Soft Drinks

When they've got a cold or flu, many people drink soft drinks, both to keep up their fluid intake and because they taste good. If you are going to do this, make certain you don't buy drinks that contain preservatives such as benzoate, or artificial flavorings such as citral or caffeine — all of which destroy some of the vitamins and minerals you need to heal infection. Better to drink juices such as orange, apple, tomato, lemon, or carrot, which *provide* extra vitamins and minerals rather than taking them away.

Cold Sores, Fever Blisters, Cankers, Herpes Simplex

I've included this discussion here, with the nutritional material, because the treatment could involve yogurt. People who are troubled by small sores in their mouths or on their lips have observed that they seem to appear when they are under emotional pressure or when their bodies are stressed by a disease such as a cold or the flu. Because it is a stress-related symptom, taking large doses of B-complex vitamins often reduces the period of time you have these sores. The antistress formula given earlier is especially good for this.

Many people get relief by applying a soft paste made by dissolving the contents of an acidophilus capsule in water. These capsules can be purchased at most health food stores and at some drug counters. Smearing acidophilus yogurt on the external sore can also be helpful, as can eating yogurt two or three times a day.

Doctors sometimes recommend applying an ointment called Orabase for sores inside the mouth. This can be bought over the counter in most drugstores. They also recommend Blistex, Neosporin, or Bacitracin for external sores. The sores usually disappear in from a few days to three weeks.

EMOTIONS AND YOUR HEALTH

In recent years medical technology has made it possible to trace the actual physiological and chemical changes that take place in our bodies when we're experiencing certain emotions. Because of our faith in science, it seems important to cite scientific evidence for the observations that healers have made for centuries concerning states of mind and physical well-being. Science serves the healer by providing a clear picture of the interrelationships between our emotions and our susceptibility to disease.

We know, for example, that emotional pressure, or stress, acts upon the hypothalamus of the brain. In turn, the hypothalamus sends chemical messages to the pituitary gland, which causes another set of glands, the adrenal glands, to secrete a substance called glucocorticoid. When large amounts of glucocorticoids are secreted, your body produces fewer antibodies that might otherwise control the viruses or bacteria causing the infection. In addition, cortisol secretions reduce inflammation—which, as we've previously noted, acts as a protective barrier, walling off the site of infection.

A relaxed state of mind can do pretty much the reverse of the stressed state of mind—that is, it allows your inner healing abilities to work at their best. Probably the best way to do this is with the grandma remedy I called "Cozying Up." But let's say you're in a situation where you can't go to bed even though you're miserable with a cold. Is there anything you can do then? The answer is yes.

Conscious Relaxation Technique

While you are at work, find a place where you can be by yourself for three to five minutes. This may be at your desk, in the rest room, or in a quiet place during a break.

Sit in a relaxed way, both feet on the floor, hands resting open in your lap. Some people wear dark glasses or hold a book or newspaper in their lap while doing this in public places so that others won't think they're sick or doing something peculiar.

Close your eyes or just gaze off into the distance. Let your jaw completely relax.

Take a deep breath, let it out easy. Do it again. And a third time.

As you let your breathing return to normal, imagine that your entire body is warm and relaxed.

You may feel warm or tingling sensations throughout your body in one or more areas. This is normal. These are sensations associated with a relaxed state of mind.

If thoughts, ideas, and feelings enter your mind which you feel you must do something about immediately, let them rest. Tell yourself that you will act upon them later, when the time comes. But now you are letting your main energies be on relaxing.

Let yourself enjoy this relaxed state for three to five minutes. Then slowly ease back into your ordinary schedule.

When you have a slight cold you may find that doing this simple relaxation exercise is the only remedy you need. Understand that in the few minutes it takes to do this exercise your immunological system is allowed to work more effectively than while you were under the pressures of your work routine. Actual healing takes place.

If this relaxation exercise seems like something you'd like to do, start practicing it at home when you are alone and uninterrupted. As simple as it seems, it does take several attempts to be able to let yourself enjoy the feelings of relaxation you can experience in this way. If you're at home there's another relaxation exercise you can do to relieve headache, congestion, and sinus pain:

Relax Away Your Symptoms

Lie flat on your back on a carpeted floor. Be sure to remove your shoes, empty your pockets, and loosen your belt. Close your eyes. Let your jaw drop open.

Take a deep breath and let it out slowly. Do this several times, until you feel your back muscles begin to relax and your spine settle into the floor.

Let your legs relax as you breathe, imagining them to be very heavy and weak. Let your buttocks relax. Your abdomen. Your chest. Your back. Your neck. Your shoulders. Your arms.

Some people like to imagine themselves floating on a cloud. Others like to imagine all their muscles turning to jelly. Others imagine lying on the warm sand at the beach. Find an image of relaxation in your life and think about it as you relax.

Now let your facial muscles relax. To do this, smile and then let the smile muscles relax. Do this several times until your face feels loose and soft.

Wrinkle your brow; let it relax. Wrinkle and relax three or four times until your forehead muscles relax. You may feel relief from tension around your cheeks and eyes, the upper and lower sinus areas, immediately. Let yourself enjoy this feeling.

If you have a headache, raise your head about a half inch from the floor. Let it relax. Lift again. Relax. Do this several times. You will feel your neck muscles begin to relax and your headache begin to fade. Enjoy these feelings, understanding that the act of enjoyment actually helps the relaxation to take place and build.

Enjoy the feelings of relaxation for five minutes or as long as you wish. Let yourself doze off if you feel like it.

When you're ready to get up, do it slowly. Be languorous and loose. Take it easy.

Once, while we were doing a workshop for a group of students at a university, one of the participants told Dr. Samuels and me about an interesting technique he used to teach himself to relax—

specifically, to solve the problem of how to let thoughts and feelings pass through his mind when he was trying to relax. He said that to him these thoughts and feelings were like a telephone ringing, and as most people will agree, a ringing telephone is extremely hard to resist. But this person reasoned that if he could learn to let a ringing telephone go unanswered he could also learn to let his thoughts and feelings go unanswered while he was trying to relax.

He started by ignoring the ringing telephone once a day. Within a week he found he could let the phone ring without feeling he was neglecting something important. (Strangely enough, he also discovered that no one ever complained that they had any difficulty reaching him.) Now when he is trying to relax and ideas or feelings enter his mind, he treats them the same way he's learned to treat the phone. Worth trying!

After you've learned these basic relaxation remedies you'll probably find yourself embellishing them. In a relaxed state you might imagine the warm rays of the sun bathing your swollen nasal passages, throat, or sinuses. Or you might imagine white blood cells enveloping and eating up viruses. Or you might imagine viruses dissolving in chemicals secreted by the mucosal tissue of your throat and nose.

The power of your imagination is not to be underrated. The parts of the brain that form images or ideas about healing can definitely stimulate the hypothalamus, which in turn masterminds the healing processes. So we have a solid physiological basis for the mind's capacity for creating both disease and health. We'll discuss how such techniques can be used as preventive measures against disease in the chapter called "Creating Health."

PHYSICAL EXERCISE

Physical exercise, which has only recently been accepted by the medical community as valuable therapy in certain kinds of cardiovascular disease, may also prove important in infectious diseases. The increased circulation of blood throughout one's body strengthens blood vessels, oxygenates more cells better, and toughens the heart muscle itself. People in their later years who have suffered heart attacks or strokes discover themselves in incredibly good health after a few months in medically supervised rehabilitation programs, sometimes reporting complete freedom from chronic diseases, such as colds, which had plagued them throughout their lives.

There are many well-documented cases of people in their later years who are now running marathon races of 20 miles and more after having been told by their doctors that they had heart disease —and who have never before enjoyed better health.

The healing that goes on in one's body with vigorous exercise is profound. But research to establish why it is so profound has only begun. There are a number of things we do know about it, however, and these are worth noting. First, we know that by increasing the body's metabolic rate, as we do with regular exercise, we increase, also, the activity of white blood cells throughout our body. Thus the immunological system works at its peak, and white blood cells, which devour foreign substances, are encouraged to speed up their work.

Moreover, people who regularly exercise—walking, jogging, swimming, or cycling a half hour or more per day—experience a sense of emotional well-being and self-confidence that is psychologically satisfying. Part of this response, some endocrinologists speculate, may be due to the hormone called norepinephrine—this substance, you'll recall, is produced when you exercise and has a psychic effect as well as a physical one. With even small amounts of this hormone, people experience a sense of deep happiness and even euphoria. Another benefit of exercise may be that we feel confidence in our body when we know we can run a mile or two or many more without getting exhausted or sick in the process. It is my opinion that every cell in your body responds to this confidence.

As we noted in the discussion of relaxation, your mental states affect your resistance to infection. The emotions you experience, both from hormones and from accomplishment, when you get into a regular program of exercise, are emotions conducive to health. Moreover, people who exercise regularly sleep better, are better able to relax, and have generally more energy than their more sedentary peers.

A RELEVANT BIT OF PERSONAL HISTORY

During the year I wrote this book I had more colds than I'd had in five years. I attribute a good part of that to the wet winter, which cut into my usual routine of cycling in the mountains near my home. At the age of thirty-five I began cycling a couple of miles every day. Five years later I think nothing of doing 40 or more miles in a day, with an average of 75 miles every week — and this in extremely hilly terrain.

I know that my resistance to disease is directly linked to my exercise routine. If the routine is broken, as mine was this winter, the number of colds I get immediately climbs. I sleep poorly. I overeat. I have less energy, and I am tense and moody. Having read dozens of interviews and letters from people who enjoy regular exercise programs, I am convinced that my experiences are by no means unique.

If you are a person who doesn't exercise and who suffers numerous colds through the fall and winter months, consider starting a regular exercise program. If you've dropped a program of exercise recently, go back to it, starting at about half to three-quarters of what you were doing when you left off. As you build up to your previous capacities, see if the number of colds you get isn't reduced. If it's cold and wet outside, try exercises such as sit-ups, running in place, or stationary cycling, working at five-minute intervals if you're a beginner, up to a half hour if you're accustomed to more vigorous exercise.

If you have a cold now, how can exercise help you? Though you won't feel much like it, go out and take a brisk walk, even if you have a slight fever. Walk a half mile if you're not accustomed to it, a mile or two if you have been exercising regularly. See if it doesn't make you feel better almost immediately.

HOW TO GET THE BENEFITS OF EXERCISE WHEN YOU CAN'T

When I have a cold or flu I find that I get relief from congestion and tightness in my chest by approximating some of the experiences of rigorous exercise. I sit in a straight-backed chair with both feet flat on the floor, hands folded in my lap. Then I relax myself, using the technique I described in the previous section. When I'm completely relaxed I imagine myself riding my bicycle on my favorite ride. I picture my favorite turns, downhills and uphills, and imagine how it feels to ride through them. Sometimes pictures, as in daydreams, come to mind. Sometimes I feel bodily sensations like the ones I get on a real ride.

When I have the imaginary ride established in my mind, I take three or four deep, heavy breaths, exhaling and inhaling as I would on a hard ride up a very steep hill. But I never take more than three or four such breaths. Then I relax, letting my breath return to normal, as I feel my heart momentarily beat a little faster and feel the effects of increased oxygenation that the breathing produces. I may repeat this breathing exercise as much as six times, but seldom more than that. Immediately afterward I experience relief from the tense, tight feelings of congestion. Many of the aches and pains associated with upper respiratory infection are relieved. For a while I feel pretty good again.

It may be useful to explore why this imaginary exercise works. The breathing helps, of course, because it does approximate some of the effects of hard physical exercise on your body. But in addition, we are using the imagination to stimulate changes within the body that are experienced with real exercise — hormonal changes, blood flow, acid levels, and all the rest.

Everyone has had experiences which prove that thoughts, ideas, and feelings can cause physiological changes. Being reminded of an embarrassing moment can cause your cheeks to flush, which is brought about by hormones that cause tiny blood vessels to open. Imagining a sensuous experience can cause changes in your genitals associated with sexual arousal. Or perhaps you've imagined yourself in a frightening situation and suddenly discovered that your palms were sweating.

So physiological changes brought about by things you imagine are common experiences for everyone. Next time you're reading a tensely plotted book or watching a terrifying movie, take note of how the emotions you feel are being manifested in your body. You may discover increased heart and respiration rates. You may discover yourself sweating. But it is almost certain that you'll discover you are seemingly involuntarily tensing the muscles of your arms, legs, back, abdomen, and neck. Your jaw muscles may be tight and you may be making a fist. These are normal responses to threatening situations, responses that are often so automatic we're hardly aware of them.

My imagined bicycle ride does not have as profound effects on my body as the real thing but it does result in actual physiological changes. These changes provide me with some of the benefits of real exercise: increased circulation, relaxation of muscles in the upper part of the body, a slight elevation in body temperature, and quite likely an increased antibody production.

HOW TO USE ACUPRESSURE TO RELIEVE CONGESTION

Not long ago acupuncture was a highly controversial subject in the medical community. But now nearly every large medical clinic or hospital has its resident acupuncture expert and is applying this ancient medical technique in a number of ways, ranging from treatment for lower backache to anesthesia. Why acupuncture works is not exactly known but it is clear that it does work in the treatment of a variety of human diseases. One of the best things about it is that it gets results without any known side effects. The treatment actually improves the total organism.

Acupressure is based on the same principles as acupuncture, but since it requires no needles, you can do it yourself without the need for paraphernalia and special skills. Acupressure is applied with your fingertips. It is a simple matter of pressing on areas of your body with the padded part of your fingertip using just the right

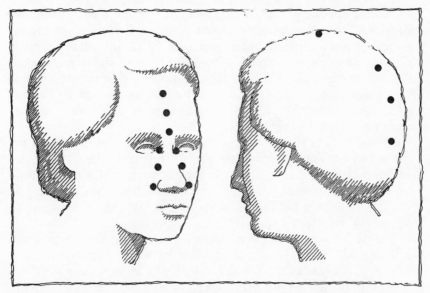

Figure 8: Acupressure or Shiatsu. Press fingers firmly but gently on dots and move in small circles about two or three cycles per second. Press on the matching points to the right and left of the nose at the same time. Your hands should be warm when doing this.

amount of pressure. How much pressure is just the right amount? The right amount is halfway between pleasure and pain. Since the treatment I describe here is self-applied, it will be easy to judge for yourself when you have the right pressure.

This simple treatment brings immediate though temporary relief from sinus pain and headaches often associated with a cold or flu. Here's how it works.

Each of the dots in Figure 8 represents a point to press. Start in the center of your face and then work downward, pressing firmly with your right index finger on your right side, left finger on the left side. Work down to your nostrils, pressing each point no more than three to five seconds.

When you have done the points alongside your nose, go back and and begin with the pressure points working from between your eyebrows up, again giving each point a three to five second pressure. Now press the point on the top of your head, followed by the last three points as noted.

UNDERSTANDING THE DOCTOR'S MAGIC

Strictly speaking a discussion of going to the doctor probably doesn't belong in a chapter on self-treatment. But for some people there is a kind of magic about going to the doctor when they are sick. In a strange way the visit itself is a form of self-treatment. In the case of colds and flu, it has been estimated that visits for respiratory disease account for more than half the business of the general practitioner — this in spite of the fact that doctors have little to offer their patients with colds or flu.

My opinion is that people with colds and flu go to doctors for reassurance. The examination the doctor gives, and the brief verbal exchange, are important to the patient not because valuable information is exchanged or a prescription for a healing drug is written, but because the mystery of the patient's symptoms is solved. Worries are dispelled.

This is not to say that doctors never give real help for respiratory infections. If for one reason or another you weren't able to take the time to heal a cold or flu, for example, and a more serious infection has set in, the doctor can diagnose you and prescribe specific treatment to help your body get well. But the cold and flu, we all know, are different. There are no specific treatments.

Many people feel uncomfortable about accepting the idea that we need a doctor as much to ease our worries about disease as to dispense "real" medicine. But easing the patient's worry—a form of comfort, after all—is the very basis of medicine. Throughout history, and in every culture known to us, there have been physicians, shamans, medicine men, and priests whose purpose it has been to provide access to all the knowledge available, at the time, about human ills and how to correct them.

With the technical advances that have been made in medicine in the past hundred years or so, we have come to expect miracle cures for every illness we suffer. But the lay person overrates the abilities of modern medicine—and vastly underrates the important powers his or her own body possesses. On those rare occasions when a cold or flu turns to something more serious, such as a strep throat, an infected ear, or pneumonia, the miracle cures, mainly antibiotics, really can help, that's true, but without the human body's natural healing and restorative abilities, even the miracle drugs would be useless.

What does a doctor look for when he or she examines you for a cold or flu? Let's go through this process point by point, using a typical visit to a doctor's office to illustrate.

After you have read last month's news magazines in the waiting room, the nurse finally leads you into the doctor's examination room. The nurse—let's say it's a woman—puts a thermometer in your mouth, briefly takes your pulse, then makes some notes on your chart, which she fastens to a clip on the door. You may then be asked to remove your shirt—let's say you're a man—and are told the doctor will be in to examine you in a couple of minutes. After several minutes of restlessly shifting around on the crinkly paper covering the examination table, you look around for a magazine to read. Not finding any, you study the paraphernalia in the room. You consider snooping but decide against it.

Prior to the exam the doctor reads your medical chart to see if you have any previous history of lung disease, heart disease, diabetes or any other chronic illness. Since you have none of those the diagnosis is fairly simple: "Take a couple aspirin, drink plenty of fluids, and call me if you don't feel better in the next couple days."

But what if in the examination your doctor did find some problems? Let's say, for example, that you had symptoms suggesting an ear infection. Or tonsillitis. Or a strep throat infection. Or bronchitis. In any of these, the procedure would be pretty much the same. Your throat would be swabbed lightly with a cotton-tipped stick and the stick would be sent out for culturing. The culture would determine whether you had a bacterial or viral infection. Meanwhile, if you had a high fever, the doctor would prescribe antibiotics and tell you to stay home in bed—since the chances would be fairly high that you had a bacterial infection for which antibiotics are extremely helpful.

And what if you have a chronic disease in addition to the cold or flu? Depending on your doctor, the treatment provided would not be much different than that prescribed for a person with no chronic disease. But the doctor would want to watch you more closely to make certain that your body was doing an adequate job of both healing and resisting further infection.

After you leave the doctor's office you may feel a combination of relief and disappointment: relief to discover that your illness isn't serious, disappointment to discover that the doctor could not prescribe an instant cure. The examination was done quickly but with confidence, and you feel secure about the medical attention you've received.

Of course, after all this you still have to heal the cold, and the doctor has probably offered little or nothing in the way of advice about how to do that. So what, you may ask, has been accomplished in this visit? Perhaps only one thing—the doctor's diagnosis has provided you with reassurance that what you have is really a cold or flu and nothing more serious. With your worry gone, you can go home, snuggle up in bed with your copy of *Cold Comfort*, and put together your own self-treatment program.

PUTTING IT ALL TOGETHER

You now have a number of medical tools—that is, knowledge, techniques, and recipes for remedies—to assemble an intelligent self-treatment program for yourself the next time you have a cold or the flu. In addition to actual treatment techniques, you also have (from your study of the earlier part of the book) a solid understanding of how both infection and healing take place in your body.

I like to think of these things as tools, or more precisely, as "mental tools," since like a wrench, pen, spatula, or computer, they expand our natural capacities and allow us to have greater control of our lives. In my own mind, I like to imagine a little black bag, the traditional symbol of the general practitioner, filled to overflowing with the mental tools described in *Cold Comfort*.

If you've got poetic leanings you might now remember the self-practitioner idea we discussed in the second chapter. In your mind's eye you might imagine that your self-practitioner now carries a little black bag of mental tools. He or she is well equipped to diagnose and treat you. To round out your self-practitioner's medical education, you need to know more about over-the-counter cold pills, as well as some of the other more potent drugs available for colds, flu, and their complications. That's what the next chapter is all about.

References

Mike Samuels, M.D., and Hal Z. Bennett: *The Well Body Book* (New York: Random House, 1973).
Linus Pauling: *Vitamin C, the Common Cold and the Flu* (New York: Bantam, 1973).
Roger J. Williams, M.D.: *Nutrition Against Disease* (New York: Bantam, 1973).
Mark Bricklin: *Natural Healing* (Emmaus, Pa.: Rodale Press, 1976).
Adelle Davis: *Let's Get Well* (New York: Signet, 1965).
N. W. Walker: *Diet and Salad* (Phoenix: Norwalk Press, 1940).

Chapter Seven

Drugs and Upper Respiratory Infections

This chapter explores the contents and effects of the most commonly used over-the-counter cold remedies. We'll be discussing benefits as well as dangers and side effects, in detail, for everything from antihistamines to aspirin. We'll be looking at when and how to use these drugs, as well as how not to use them. More than a pharmacopoeia, this chapter provides you with the knowledge to make intelligent judgments about common drugs offered for the treatment of colds, flu, and their complications.

Let's begin this discussion with some general comments about cold pills. Then we'll consider each separate drug and its effects on the healing processes in greater detail.

According to the *Harvard Medical School Newsletter* (January 1978), we spend more than $500 million per year for over-the-counter cold remedies—and this does not include aspirin! In most cases the drugs do little or nothing to reduce the discomfort of the common cold or the flu. And no drug cures either one.

Symptoms, though, are sometimes changed by cold pills—that is, one discomfort is reduced at the expense of creating a new one as a *side effect* of the drug taken. So one might well ask: What are these second symptoms, and am I any better off with them than I was with the untreated cold? Too often the answer will be that you are paying for drugs that will either complicate your flu or cold, or do nothing at all for it.

Consider the following from the 1967 edition of *Current Therapy*, a standard reference book for practicing physicians:

> In this age of miracle drugs it is often difficult to accept the fact that no specific treatment is available for viral infections of the respiratory tract. . . . This knowledge, and the fact that all drugs may under certain circumstances have undesirable side effects, indicate that fluids, cold mist, aspirin, reassurance, and observation should be chief therapeutic agents employed in the treatment of most acute viral infections of the respiratory tract.

And in *The Dangerous Cold,* on the subject of antihistamines, Noah Fabricant says:

> No allergy treatment or cure, such as an antihistamine, can have any positive effect on common-cold viruses. . . .
> They have no place at all in a "shotgun-type" cold-cure pill or capsule. They are simply a waste of your money and, quite possibly, a hazard to your alertness and general "tone."

The same writer, on ephedrine drugs, sold as one of the ingredients in cold pills to "shrink swollen nasal membranes," tells us: "For one thing, once its effect has worn off, the congestion returns — often worse than ever."

Important medical studies have been published, and made widely available to physicians, which demonstrate that antihistamines are, at the very least, ineffective in the treatment of cold and flu symptoms. A study in the *New England Journal of Medicine* in 1950 showed that antihistamines can have a "placebo" effect for some people. But these medications do not in any positive way change the course of the infection. Another study in the *Medical Letter* in 1971 refutes the claims of those drug companies who tell us that their inclusion of antihistamines in cold pills suppresses your cough.

If simple ineffectiveness of the widely advertised cold remedies was the only problem we faced with these preparations, we might be willing to look the other way in the widespread marketing of these pills — especially since a placebo effect can be a real enough form of comfort. Unfortunately, ineffectiveness is not the only issue here.

Every drug company, dictated by federal law, must publish, and make widely available to every physician, a list of the side effects of every drug made and marketed in the United States. Periodically, this information is published in a large book called *Physician's*

Desk Reference (*PDR* for short). Moreover, a description of side effects must be included in all over-the-counter preparations.

It has been my experience, however, that only a few physicians or patients take the time to study these side effects. We perhaps neglect to do so because we don't take the "cure" any more seriously than we take the disease. The attitude that "It's just a cold or the flu" transposes easily to "It's just a cold pill." But the side effects can be detrimental to your health and can either prolong your illness or make it more serious.

Obviously there are doctors who are in fact concerned about side effects and who do make a point of understanding them. When they recommend the use of antihistamines and ephedrines in treating the symptoms of upper respiratory infections, they are careful to warn that "medications used to treat this symptom may eventually aggravate the condition." (The quotation is from *Current Therapy 1973.*)

An article in *Current Diagnosis and Treatment 1965* gives a particularly clear and complete description of the common side effects of cold pills. The following evaluation provides a good set of criteria for anyone who wishes to make an educated choice between the symptoms of an untreated cold or flu and the symptoms created by a drug one might take to *treat* that same cold or flu:

> Therapeutic doses cause a high incidence of toxic reactions, including drowsiness, dryness of the mouth, headache, nausea, tachycardia [irregular heartbeat], blurred vision, constipation, tinnitus [ringing in the ears], skin rash, urinary retention, and nervousness.

Constant use of antihistamines — that is, over a period of years or months — has been found to cause a condition called *agranulocytosis*. This means that the production of white blood cells is reduced or stopped in your body. Since white blood cells are essential in your natural defense against infection and disease, it is not a condition to be taken lightly.

We should note here that agranulocytosis is an extremely rare side effect of cold pills, occurring only under unusual circumstances: either from extremely high dosages or from the combination of high dosages taken over a period of months or years. Yet it is worth considering these dramatic effects because doing so makes it quite clear that these popularly used drugs are both powerful and potentially harmful.

DRUGS: BENEFITS AND SIDE EFFECTS

Aspirin†
Intended benefits: Reduces aches and pains caused by inflammation.
Reduces fever.
Potential side effects: From overuse—burning sensations in throat and
mouth; upset stomach, difficulty breathing, dizziness, ringing ears.
If you have ulcers—don't use aspirin because it dissolves tissue. Long
term use—can cause anemia due to low level internal bleeding. Re-
duces thrombin production—your body produces thrombin to co-
agulate blood, and thus aspirin can impair your ability to heal cuts.
Extremely large amounts—can cause death, especially in children.

*Aspirin substitutes: N-phenylacetamide, phenacetin, acetophenatidin,
acetaminophen, p-hydroxyacetanilide†*
Intended benefits: Reduces aches and pains, and reduces fever (with
some). Basically replaces aspirin for people who are allergic to it.
Potential side effects: Liver and kidney damage, fall in blood pressure,
respiratory failure.

Antihistamine†
Intended benefits: Reduces the body's natural secretion of histamines,
the fluids that cause what is commonly called inflammation.
Potential side effects: Drowsiness, depression, anxiety, moodiness, upset
stomach, thirst, dry cough, tightness in chest, constipation. Effects
are increased by use of alcohol. Constricts small blood vessels. Long
term use—reduction of white blood cell production.

Decongestants and Nasal Sprays or Drops†
Intended benefits: Reduces secretions of histamines.
Potential side effects: Can cause "rebound" effect, that is, increased production of histamines. Irritates linings of nose and throat. Can change
acid balance of respiratory system, opening it to infection. Constricts
blood vessels. Some experts believe these drugs can prolong a cold or
flu. Mood changes as in antihistamines. Naphazoline and tetrahy-
drozoline are known to cause unconsciousness in children.

Cold Pills or Drug Stews
Intended Benefits: Cold pills are advertised as easing all the discomforts
of colds and flu. Most of these drugs are combinations of ingredients
such as aspirin, antihistamines, decongestants, and/or aspirin substitutes. Many contain caffeine in large amounts to overcome drowsiness
caused by antihistamines.
Potential side effects: Add up all the side effects caused by the drugs contained in cold pills. These compounds usually contain both stimulants
and depressants and may alter moods and cause a feeling of confusion.

†May be contained in cold pills or other over-the-counter drugs.

Where colds and the flu are concerned there are specific side effects—even in the moderate use of cold remedies—that can make your symptoms much worse and thus prolong your discomfort. You ought to be aware of such effects if you want to reduce the negative influence of colds and flu in your life. Now let's start our more detailed examination of drugs with aspirin since it is included in so many treatment programs for colds and flu.

ASPIRIN

Aspirin is one of the oldest and most commonly used over-the-counter pain-relieving drugs. As such, it is effective and relatively safe if used discriminately. One or two tablets, taken no more often than every four hours, can reduce the inflammation that causes headaches and aches in your muscles and joints when you have a cold or the flu.

We know that aspirin is included in many cold pills. But sometimes people take the pills without thinking about this, and since they know that aspirin helps relieve discomfort and mild fever, they take, in addition to the cold pills, a couple aspirin every few hours. Doing so can cause low-level aspirin poisoning.

Even low-level aspirin poisoning can produce physical effects you may think are symptoms of your cold. These are: stinging or burning sensations in your throat and mouth; upset stomach; difficulty breathing; slight dizziness; and ringing ears. The fact that these side effects are close to what you'd ordinarily associate with cold symptoms is important. In other words, you may, if you have been taking cold pills along with aspirin, notice a reduction in your symptoms when you stop taking the so-called remedies.

At the risk of overdramatizing our case, it is interesting to note that although aspirin is considered to be a mild drug, it is responsible for poisoning many children each year. The fruit flavoring used in some preparations encourages children to eat them like candy, resulting either in death or serious toxic reactions affecting vital organs. Aspirin should be kept out of the reach of children.

Since concentrations of aspirin are capable of disolving healthy tissue, it is always recommended that aspirin be taken with food, milk, or plenty of warm liquids. When taken this way, the aspirin mixes with the food or liquid, thus diluting it and preventing the pill from sitting in one part of your stomach to eat away at healthy tissue. (Bleeding ulcers have been known to be caused, or seriously aggravated, by the use of aspirin.)

Aspirin can also cause anemia, brought on by small amounts of internal bleeding — one of the usual side effects of this common drug. It is a well-known medical fact that even one aspirin will greatly reduce your body's ability to produce thrombin, a necessary ingredient in the blood's normal coagulating processes. For this reason, careful surgeons will warn their patients against taking aspirin for at least seven days before surgery, since even one aspirin taken during that time can prolong bleeding.

Moreover, aspirin causes a fall in blood sugar and thus can be responsible for feelings of lethargy and depression when you take it for a prolonged period.

Recently, physicians have taken a more conservative approach to the long-standing tradition of "take two aspirins and drink plenty of fluids." The *Merck Manual* for 1977 now warns us that aspirin causes the infected person to become more contagious; because of this many physicians believe that the use of this medication should be limited to cold or flu sufferers who will not be subjecting others to their infection.

What about the so-called aspirin substitutes? (The names to look for are N-phenylacetamide, phenacetin, acetophenetidin, acetaminophen, p-hydroxyacetanilide.) Most researchers agree that aspirin substitutes should be used only by people who have severe sensitivities to aspirin — and then only with extreme caution. The potential side effects listed are: liver and kidney damage; fall in blood pressure; respiratory failure. Since most of the side effects of aspirin will disappear within a short period after discontinuing their use, and the damage of some aspirin substitutes will not, most people will want to stick with aspirin.

One thing you should remember when taking even regular small doses of aspirin for a cold is that they do accomplish what they claim to accomplish as a pain reducer. In this respect they mask your symptoms, and since you do feel better you may continue to work when you should be resting and taking care of yourself. Remember: The cold or flu will continue to follow its natural course. The aspirin won't change that. Chances are you're better off saying to your body: "Okay, I'll rest until the pain goes away." More often than not this is the tactic that will shorten the duration of your cold or flu.

ANTIHISTAMINES

Normally the tissue of your throat, upper nasal passages, and sinuses is moist and warm. These areas secrete moisture constantly, which creates a cleansing and filtering action.

Histamines are produced by your own body as a normal, healthy response to tissue damage. As virus activity kills cells in your nose and throat, the histamines are released. These, in turn, stimulate increased blood flow to the damaged area by causing small blood vessels to expand. Increased blood flow is important when you are injured or ill, since the blood cleanses the area, carries nutrients for repair, and fights further infection. The histamines your body produces are messengers to your body, asking that those healing activities take place.

When histamines are produced, fluids are also released into the damaged area of your body. The fluids are meant to bathe the area, to wash away dead cells, and to wall off the infected or damaged areas and isolate them from healthy areas of your body. Unfortunately, the fluid activity, called inflammation, presses on nerve endings, resulting in pain. It is most often in response to this single complaint that people find themselves taking antihistamines. Understand, however, that antihistamines in medicines block normal healing functions. The prefix "anti," I believe, best describes their relationship to your normal healing processes.

But there are still other side effects. In fact, there are a great many of them. Let's say you've got a cold or the flu and you've taken a couple of cold pills. An hour or so later, you begin to feel drowsy, depressed, moody, and a little sick to your stomach. You think these symptoms are caused by the flu or cold, but a careful evaluation may prove them to be caused by the antihistamines in the cold pill you took! Let's say you don't know that. You just attribute these feelings to the cold or flu. They are, after all, discomforts you have learned to associate with colds and flu. So you continue taking the remedy.

The next day you have a cough. Your mouth feels dry. You feel tight in the chest. Your hands feel heavy and weak. To add insult to injury, you're constipated. More cold or flu symptoms? Not necessarily. All these effects can also be reactions to antihistamines. If you stopped taking the cold pills, you'd have only the discomfort of your cold or flu — and maybe you'd feel better.

NASAL SPRAYS AND DECONGESTANTS

Nasal sprays and decongestants have many of the same effects on your body as antihistamines. In addition they inhibit or paralyze the tiny cilia activity within the mucosal tissue of your nose and upper respiratory tract. The cilia, which are microscopic hairs, normally have a sort of swimming action that keeps fluids and microscopic particles moving away from healthy cells. This part of your cleansing mechanism is greatly inhibited or even stopped by the ingredients of nasal sprays and decongestants.

Moreover, these medications cause the acid-base balance of your nose to change. Where there should be acidity there is now alkalinity. It has been demonstrated that a specific acid level is necessary for optimum health and resistance to infection. When your nasal passages become too alkaline, that alkalinity invites disease. It provides a medium that encourages viruses to multiply.

What all this adds up to is that nasal decongestants or sprays, which give only brief relief at best, can change the environment within your nasal passages so that you are opening yourself up to further infection and thus increased discomfort.

DRUG STEWS CAN BE
HAZARDOUS TO YOUR HEALTH

Most cold pills are a combination of drugs — what I call "drug stews." One that I looked at recently had an antihistamine, a decongestant, aspirin, an aspirin substitute, plus a liberal dose of caffeine! Drug companies mix up these stews mainly as a marketing device. How many times have you heard the ad that claims such things as "more active ingredients than the leading cold pill" or "a combination of medically active ingredients"? But the truth of the matter is that this penchant for drug stews, this shotgun approach to treating symptoms, is no more effective than any one of the ingredients included in those compounds.

Some of the active ingredients act as stimulants in your body while others act as depressants. Some increase blood flow to some areas while others decrease that flow. Your body is being given so many mixed messages it's a wonder it doesn't rebel. Maybe it does!

Do you feel jittery, nervous, hyperactive, emotionally sensitive, and restless? This could be caused by the caffeine they put in your cold pills to counteract the drowsiness caused by the antihistamine.

Or it could be the ephedrine put in the pill to relieve the discomfort of congestion. Or it could be your body's own unique reaction to all those drugs taken in combination.

By now my message is clear. Avoid these drug stews. Far better that you live with the clear-cut, normal, everyday symptoms of the virus infection than confuse your body with these peculiar substances. Remember: Your body clearly understands how to handle the cold or flu. But it's questionable how well it knows how to handle all the chemical substances with which we bombard ourselves when we take "the leading cold pill."

ANTIBIOTICS

Antibiotic drugs go under a variety of generic names: penicillin, sulfonamide, erythromycin, tetracycline. The word "antibiotic" literally means "against life," so named because the drugs that come under this heading are designed to destroy certain kinds of living microorganisms present with infections. They destroy bacteria but they do not destroy viruses.

Although this is somewhat of an oversimplification, antibiotics kill or stop the spread of bacteria in your body just as spray bombs and chemical strips reduce the insect population in your house. Generally, the antibiotic is not dangerous to you, though it will destroy microorganisms or prevent them from reproducing.

Using antibiotics in treating colds and the flu is foolish, if not dangerous, for at least four reasons. In the first place, viruses that cause colds are not affected by antibiotics. Second, antibiotics, in addition to destroying harmful bacteria, also destroy helpful bacteria such as vitamin K, which lives in your intestines and is absolutely essential to your health. Third, many people are allergic to antibiotics, especially penicillin, with reactions ranging from skin rash to death from respiratory failure. And fourth, certain strains of bacteria develop new generations of their kind that are resistant to antibiotics — the result now being recognized, worldwide, as bacterial infections that are not affected by antibiotic treatment.

Whereas it was once not uncommon to prescribe antibiotics for flu and colds, most medical books now strongly warn against this practice, often using phrases such as "the use of antibiotics for the treatment of the common cold is deplorable." Consider the following observation from *Current Therapy 1973:*

Antibacterial agents should not be used in acute viral infections, for they have no antiviral action. There is no evidence that they prevent bacterial complications of acute viral respiratory infections and they may, in fact, encourage the emergence of resistant organisms. In addition, serious toxic or allergic reactions to these potent drugs may occur. The patient may be sensitized to the antibacterial drug and thus be denied the use of an important therapeutic agent during a subsequent serious bacterial infection.

A good rule of thumb is to ask any doctor who prescribes antibiotics for your cold or flu why he or she believes this to be necessary. Ask them if they suspect the presence of a bacterial (rather than a viral) infection. If they do not, tell them you understand that antibiotics don't work for viral infections.

Bacterial complications following a cold or a bout with the flu can be serious, and this is the time for effective treatment with antibiotics. Strep throat, some ear infections, pneumonia, bronchitis, laryngitis, and even sinus infections can be caused by bacteria. When a doctor has good reason to suspect these conditions, then a prescription for antibiotics may be helpful. But make the doctor explain exactly why the drug is being recommended for your use.

Too often patients who demand this kind of accurate and responsible medical service discover that the doctor has prescribed the antibiotics for one of two reasons: either as a preventive measure (which as we have seen is a useless practice) or to make patients feel they are getting their money's worth, even though the antibiotic could not possibly have anything more than a placebo effect.

Use antibiotics only when there is reasonable evidence that you have a bacterial infection. Remember that they have no effect on cold and flu viruses.

NO TRUTH IN ADVERTISING

But what about the promises of relief made in cold pill ads? Some say the art of television has progressed nowhere further than in advertising. When I watch the ads for cold remedies, I am more than convinced this is true. Images of miserable-looking people with handkerchiefs clutched to their noses, cartoon hammers or clamps pressing in on the sides of a person's head, people's faces dissolving, a cough that causes a karate expert to lose control and break up furniture — all these have become firmly implanted in my mind, thanks to television.

I think it would be interesting to make a study of television commercials for cold remedies and see if they had any subtle, subliminal effects on people's health. It's a farfetched idea, I'll admit. But when I spoke to several friends about this matter, asking them how they felt when they watched cold pill commercials, most of them agreed that some literally made them feel like they were getting the symptoms the ads depicted.

I'm sure there's at least an element of truth in this suspicion. Still, the more important issue, at this point, has to do with the relief the ads promise and simply cannot deliver. As Dr. Noah Fabricant puts it: "Here we want to emphasize that it is the advertising, whether in television or radio, newspapers or magazines, that does most to mislead and confuse people on the merit of these medications."

If there is one fact worth knowing about how cold remedies affect your body, it is that most of them have the potential to cause discomfort equal to, or even worse than, the cold or flu itself. I wonder how many of us have suffered through days of discomfort that we attributed to a cold or flu but was actually caused by cold pills!

Since medical scientists largely agree that no cold remedies *cure* anything, and any benefits derived from them can only be negligible, we really have nothing to lose by avoiding these drugs altogether. One thing is certain — most ingredients in cold pills interfere with the normal healing processes of the human body. This strongly suggests to me that it can take longer to get over an infection treated with cold pills than to get over one for which you took no medication whatsoever.

WHEN DRUGS CAN HELP

In spite of my warnings about the side effects of cold pills, I believe there are times when they can be helpful. Aspirin, for example, is safe for people who are either not allergic to it or who do not experience upset stomach when taking it. Its therapeutic benefits are numerous: It can reduce inflammation and thus reduce pain. It can lower fever, and even act as an anticoagulant for people with certain kinds of cardiovascular disease.

My position on aspirin is that it should be highly respected by anyone considering its use. Literally hundreds of tons of aspirin are consumed by the American public each year, leading one to conclude not only that it is a big industry but, even more important, that it is being used indiscriminately, undoubtedly encouraged by advertising. Just as with any other powerful drug, the indiscriminate use of aspirin, as we've discussed several times in this book, can actually get in the way of your body's own self-healing processes — processes far more complex and far more effective than any therapeutic technique ever devised by the human mind.

Nevertheless, there are times, in the normal course of some flu infections, for example, when a fever-caused headache makes you so uncomfortable and anxious that it may warrant the use of aspirin to bring relief. At such times, I feel, the stress caused by the headache may impede the healing process more than the aspirin would. (Along with aspirin, I like to take a multivitamin pill containing vitamins A, B complex, and C.) In other words, by taking aspirin, which reduces fever and inflammation, you can achieve a degree of comfort in an hour or less, comfort that has its own therapeutic benefits.

There are medical people who propose that aspirin be assigned to the "prescription only" list. I am strongly opposed to this. In my ideal society, which is not exactly around the corner, medical education for all people would replace government policing of drugs and practitioners. Each of us would accept full responsibility for our own body, and if the government were to have any part in my plan that part would be to help publish and disseminate medical information so that all people could make intelligent, individual decisions about health.

But the fact that some people want to put aspirin on the prescription list does indicate that I'm not the only one who feels the need to reevaluate this drug and learn to respect its power. As it is now, aspirin is marketed and used as freely as candy. Before I use this or any other drug, I want to learn about both its positive and its negative powers, and from that knowledge I will make my own decisions about its use.

Another drug I think can sometimes be used to one's advantage is a decongestant. The most common of these, and the one most easily available, is Sudafed, sold over the counter in most drugstores and even in some supermarkets.

As I mentioned elsewhere in this book, one of my sons has had a history of getting earaches along with his colds. The earaches are caused when his eustachian tubes become congested. When this happens, the inner ear becomes like a pool with no outlet, a cul-de-sac, and in this stagnant state there is a high potential for infection. In the early stage of a cold he takes one aspirin and one decongestant dosage, not more than twice a day. Along with these, he takes a gram or two of vitamin C. This simple treatment helps keep his eustachian tubes open and thus reduces the chances for ear infection to occur.

It has been our experience that this treatment is more effective than the antibiotics which doctors have administered in the past. When I mentioned this fact to one of my doctor friends, he explained why this was probably true: Antibiotics are carried through the bloodstream to the site of infection, and since the inner ear has only a minuscule blood vessel network to serve it, the chances of pumping enough antibiotics to the infection are practically nil. The decongestant, aspirin, and vitamin C, however, do their work in the fleshy areas around the eustachian tubes, an area where the blood supply is rich.

Again, as with aspirin, respect for the use of any drug is essential. The intelligent self-practitioner weighs his or her knowledge of the potential negative side effects against the potential benefits. Whenever careful deliberation suggests that the drug can actually *aid* the healing processes, rather than simply impeding them, that's the time to consider its use.

References

C. Alan Phillips, M.D.: *Current Therapy* (Philadelphia: Saunders, 1967).
Noah Fabricant, M.D.: *The Dangerous Cold* (New York: Macmillan, 1965).
Merck Manual of Diagnosis and Therapy, 13th edition (Rahway, N.J.: Merck, 1978).
Sander Institute: *Influenza: Virus, Vaccines and Strategy* (New York: Academic Press, 1976).

Chapter Eight

Creating Health:
The Step Beyond Prevention

This chapter tells you how to take an increasingly effective role in your own health care. We now go beyond the subjects of the diagnosis and treatment of colds and the flu, and enter the general area of creating health. Here we explore a number of subjects—including vaccination, nutrition, exercise, and changes in the physical environment—that are aimed at improving health in a broad way. The more vigorous one's general health, the more resistant that person will be to cold and flu infections. The benefits of applying the material in this chapter will ultimately be enjoyed not only as increased mental and physical comfort but also in reduced health care costs.

Let's begin this chapter with some general comments on the subject of prevention. Then, as we go into greater detail, I will both criticize some existing techniques and offer a few alternatives. Finally, we'll get into the concept of *creating* health, a medical approach that goes one step beyond both prevention and healing. Throughout your reading of this chapter, bear in mind that by improving your total health, in a way that may seem very broad at first, you build resistance to cold and flu infections.

The subject of prevention is a controversial one, especially where the common cold and flu are concerned. Some physicians argue that in the case of the common cold, research has shown there to be "no effective preventive measures at this time." However, one should carefully examine the evidence upon which such statements are made. Does it mean that *all* methods of prevention have been tried and found lacking? Obviously not. In that case, what has been tested, and on what do the doctors base their opinions? In studying the medical literature, one finds that only a few specific, drug-related preventive measures have been tested. For example, the *Merck Manual* (11th edition) states that alkalies and glycol aerosols have been tested and found useless for the prevention of the common cold.

As an interesting historical note on this general theme, in the first quarter of this century sniffing chlorine gas was thought to have both preventive and curative benefits for the common cold sufferer. This treatment was tried once by President Calvin Coolidge, and one reporter summed up the experiment thusly: "Choking and gasping he vowed never to try it again—a vow which he kept."

In addition to drugs and gases, doctors have, of course, tried vaccinating people to prevent colds and flu. Although this technique has proved somewhat effective, in some cases, against influenza, it has not proved effective with the common cold. On another subject altogether, an antiviral substance called amantadine has been demonstrated to be effective for protection against a single strain of flu (type A2, or Asian flu). But again, it is effective with only that one flu strain, and it has no effect whatsoever on the common cold.

More recently, as we noted earlier in the book, scientists have experimented with interferon, synthesized from tears and given in large doses to laboratory animals. Although the work with interferon has been interesting, such treatment is still prohibitively expensive for humans—to say nothing of the fact that it has not been thoroughly tested.

Where the vitamin C controversy is concerned, it appears that some inroads are being made regarding acceptance by the medical establishment. In the *Merck Manual* (13th edition), for example, it is conceded that: "People taking as much as 8 grams on the first day of getting a cold both had reduced severity of symptoms and a cold lasting for a shorter duration."

From an examination of all this information, one can only say that prevention through these various limited methods has proved either ineffective or of limited value. It is my contention that if we want to find an effective means of preventing the common cold and flu we must look outside these methods. But where do we look?

Well, more and more doctors are adopting the view that one's life-style is a major influence on health. Few of us find it easy to accept the notion that we ourselves may be doing things to make ourselves sick, but once we do accept that premise some interesting results occur. The busy executive, for example, who has suffered from ulcers all his working life, gains control over his disease when he accepts the idea that the tight schedule he imposes on himself is contributing to his affliction. Slowly he learns how to ease up — without adversely affecting his business — and as he does so his ulcer gets better. Or let's say a middle-aged woman with a high-pressure desk job discovers that her routine is giving her high blood pressure. She accepts that this is true and finds time in her life for a medically supervised exercise program. In a few weeks she not only feels better than she has in years but her blood pressure has dropped significantly.

Granted that life-style can affect health in these so-called functional diseases, how can the same principles possibly apply to colds and flu, which involve viruses? That, exactly, is what we'll explore in this chapter.

THE DOCTOR'S OFFERING: VACCINATION

In this age when we can be guaranteed such good protection from other viral diseases like measles, tetanus, and polio, it is hard to accept that medical science has been unable to develop a vaccine to protect us fully from cold and flu viruses. But the fact remains that the vaccines tested for these most common of all diseases have proved either of questionable or limited value.

Whereas physicians in the United States tend to support vaccination as an important line of defense against flu, physicians in other countries are generally more skeptical. This difference in attitudes was dramatized during the so-called Swine Flu scare of a few years ago when the United States spent millions of dollars in a national vaccination program while the United Kingdom spent not a cent. The irony was that the feared epidemic did not later show up in either country.

The attitude of the English might well be expressed by Sir Charles H. Stuart-Harris and Geoffrey C. Schild, reporting their views in a recent book on the subject: "It must be admitted that neither vaccines afford real promise as strategic weapons for the

control of the epidemic spread of the influenza viruses." In addition
to their skepticism about vaccines for the flu, these two doctors
expressed concern that the vaccines may cause more problems than
they solve:

> Perhaps indeed it is time to issue a warning concerning the possible
> enhancement by immunization of the natural selection pressure
> upon the influenza viruses to undergo antigenic drift. Inasmuch as
> it is possible to induce antigenic drift in laboratory strains of virus
> by passaging them through immunized mice, the possibility of a
> similar effect in the field cannot be discounted.

Translated into everyday terms, this means that worldwide vaccination programs, as presently administered, may be interfering
with natural processes of reproduction and evolution in the world of
viruses. The doctors here are warning us that in our zeal to control
viruses we may, in fact, be causing new strains to develop—strains
over which we may one day discover that we have no control. Our
efforts to control existing disease may end up with our losing control altogether.

When I read a statement with the serious implications of this
one, I want to know the background and experience of the person
or persons who made it. In this case, Sir Charles H. Stuart-Harris
is the postgraduate dean of medicine at the University of Sheffield.
Geoffrey C. Schild, the coauthor, is head of the Division of Virology, National Institute for Biological Standards and Control, in
England, and formerly the director of the World Health Organization's World Influenza Centre. These are high credentials indeed!

In the meantime, the United States forges ahead with vaccination programs and research into even more astounding ways of
playing with the microbial world. In a small pamphlet entitled
Flu, published by the U.S. Department of Health, Education, and
Welfare, it was reported that a laboratory-created vaccine called
X-31 has been tested. We find that X-31 is a product of scientific
work directed by the army which involves experiments with "re-
combinant genetic materials." This rather imposing term refers to
the manipulation of the genes of cells, viruses, and bacteria. Apparently, the army scientists have succeeded in creating a new virus
in the test tube.

In view of the potential for vaccines to bring about the evolution
of new strains of viruses—viruses against which we may or may not
be able to develop effective antibodies—I frankly think it's fool-

hardy to continue widespread vaccination programs for the flu. For the same reasons, I am very much opposed to the army-sponsored projects in which scientists play God by manipulating genetic materials. When I weigh these factors against the apparently negligible benefits of widespread flu vaccination programs, I am doubly convinced that these programs are not only fiscally irresponsible but dangerous to the public health.

ENVIRONMENT AND HEALTH

Previously we discussed how viruses alone do not necessarily cause an infection and how influences within our environment can prepare our bodies to be more or less inviting to viruses that then can cause colds or flu. As stated in a recent book, *The Influenza Viruses and Influenza,* edited by Edwin D. Kilbourne: "Interaction between influenza virus and host does not occur *in vacuo,* and like other infections it is influenced by the environment in which it occurs." The environment usually influences viruses in one of two ways: either by preparing the actual host to be more receptive to the virus or by offering the virus outside climatic situations in which it best reproduces. In some cases, both these influences will be present.

Although it is impossible, in the space we have here, to exhaust this subject, I have outlined some of the more common environmental factors that can affect your health. I've chosen factors over which most people can reasonably exercise control. These, after all, are the areas where one can best take an assertive, self-directed role in a prevention program.

Environmental Factor One: Smoking

Although most people recognize the hazards to one's heart and lungs that smoking presents, not everyone has been alerted to the ways in which smoking also increases your chances of getting respiratory infections. As an irritant, cigarette smoke reduces the effectiveness of one of your body's first lines of defense against viruses and bacteria—that is, the cilia action that moves foreign particles away from your lungs and into the muscosal blanket, which then carries these particles into your stomach where they're destroyed. The cilia can literally be paralyzed by cigarette smoke! Moreover, the irritants in cigarette smoke cause your body to produce an overabundance of bronchial mucus secretions—creating a potential for fluids going into your lungs and inviting pneumonia and bronchitic infections.

Ordinarily, cilia move foreign particles away from your lungs, sinus areas, and nasal passages. Cilia push everything toward the back of your throat. The mucosal blanket takes it from there. Without vigorous—though microscopic—movement these normally damp, mucosal areas become perfect homes for viruses. With none of those waving cilia to push them out they are quite happy to take up residence and start reproducing in abundance. By stopping smoking you can restore the activity of your cilia in about a week. If you are a smoker, this is probably the first step in a prevention program for you.

Stopping smoking isn't easy, of course. There are a number of withdrawal symptoms that people must cope with in order to be free of the pharmacological dependency on nicotine. These can—but do not always—include anxiety and irritability, problems with digestion, restlessness, difficulty sleeping, and weight gain. Knowing that these symptoms are temporary, and that you will feel better in two to six weeks, will be helpful in your program to stop.

Many people are finding themselves successful in stopping smoking through the help of smoking clinics all over the country. Most of these groups use supportive techniques to help people stop —you're able to share your quitting problems with other smokers who are also stopping, and you can share insights and techniques that others have found comforting and effective. A phone call to your local Lung Association will get you the names of people to contact about smoking clinics in your neighborhood. Most doctors also have addresses of these programs.

Environmental Factor Two: Chemical Pollutants

Chemicals and gases in the air you breathe can reduce the effectiveness of your body's natural abilities to protect itself from respiratory disease. Sometimes chemicals do this by inhibiting cilia action, as with smoking, while other substances can irritate tissue or actually destroy healthy cells, and so invite infection in the same way that open wounds or abrasions do. At the lowest level, some chemical pollutants can cause dilation or contraction of tiny blood vessels lining your respiratory tract and create coldlike symptoms, such as swelling of sinuses, runny eyes, and drippy nose, which you might mistakenly assume to be a cold.

Usually, it is relatively easy to recognize a pollutant that may be causing these problems for you, but if you have been working or living around these pollutants for a number of years you may have grown so accustomed to them that you no longer notice they're there. Moreover, it should be recognized that although it may have given you no trouble at first, a cumulative effect has taken place and the chemical substance that didn't bother you last year, or last week, has suddenly become a real problem for your body.

A comprehensive list of all substances that can cause problems with your respiratory system is, of course, impossible here. But the following listing, by category, should be extremely helpful in locating pollutants that may be troubling you:

> Smog (sulfur dioxide)
> Paints and paint thinners
> Glues
> Polymer plastic solvents and finishes
> Dust in the air (from any source)
> Gases (auto exhaust, coal gas, sewage gas, tear gas)
> Cleaning fluid (carbon tetrachloride, acetone, ketones, ammonia)
> Pesticides and herbicides
> Fluorides
> Formaldehydes
> Nitrogen oxides (cobaltous chloride, fluorine, hydrogen chloride
>   and fluorides)
> Petroleum distillates (asphalt, benzine, fuel oil, gasoline, kerosene,
>   lubricants, model airplane glue, naphtha, petroleum, ether, tar)

At work there are a number of ways to meet the challenge of reducing these pollutants in your environment. Sometimes non-polluting substances can be substitutes for those that do pollute. Sometimes air filtering systems can be installed to protect the workers, and sometimes it is best for each worker to wear a face mask attached to a sophisticated air filtering system. If you are an employee you can get help with these problems either from your labor union or from the Environmental Protection Agency (a branch of the federal government) if your employer is uncooperative. Other people will find that their best and most effective route for avoiding these pollutants is to get out of the environment which presents a danger to them—that is, change jobs or move to a non-polluted area.

However you choose to do it, remember that changing the outer environment can be an important step in a prevention program. Whether you do this by removing yourself to an environment that is healthy for you, or by improving the environment you are in, or by exerting political pressure to influence other people to make environmental improvements, a healthier life-style is in the making.

Environmental Factor Three: Allergy

We have already discussed allergies in the chapter called "When Is a Cold Not?" Rather than repeat that information here, I refer you to that chapter.

Environmental Factor Four: Climate

Temperature and humidity, as we've discussed elsewhere in this book, are factors we can usually modify to effect changes for better health. To review the information on climate I refer you to the chapter called "Virus: Villain or Innocent Bystander?"

Environmental Factor Five: Nutrition

In the discussion of self-treatment, we examined how chemicals used in food production affect our ability to assimilate certain vitamins and minerals. Briefly, BHT, nitrites, benzoate of soda, and citral, used either as preservatives or as flavoring in some packaged meats, drinks, cereals, and confections, have the effect of robbing our bodies of vitamin A. Similarly, it is known that alcohol and caffeine can rob us of vitamin C and some of the B vitamins.

All of us are aware of the warnings coming from friends, magazine articles, books, and even government reports concerning the contaminants in our food. And a good many people are probably tired of hearing about it. Furthermore, it can be argued that none of these substances has yet undergone testing to determine whether or not it contributes to virus infection. But we do know that chemicals can reduce the body's general tone and resistance to infection of all kinds.

There is, I believe, a tendency to overestimate the dangers of chemical contaminants used in the routine processing and packaging of our food. But enough evidence has been turned up, and continues to be revealed, which would indicate that we should take a cautious look at the foods we eat. A plan for prevention, a program for maximum health and resistance to disease, would be remiss without a discussion of these matters.

A conservative but intelligent approach to this problem is simply to begin reading the labels on foods more carefully. In my family we generally avoid foods with anything on the label we can't pronounce or know to be a nonnutritive substance. This approach spares one the anxiety of trying to keep up with the most current reports and rumors about the hazards of food processing chemicals. This does not mean, in our case, that we competely give up foods with these substances in them. Our chief goal is to reduce our intake of nonnutritive substances to an absolute minimum without making a full-time career of doing so.

I also believe in providing each adult member of my family with a very high quality vitamin supplement, taken two or three times a week and containing the following:

Vitamin A — 10,000 I.U.	Folic acid — 200 mg
B1 — 5 to 10 mg	Vitamin D — 400 I.U.
B2 — 5 to 10 mg	Vitamin E — 200 I.U.
Niacin — 15 mg	Calcium — 200 mg
B6 — 5 to 10 mg	Magnesium — 30 mg
Pantothenic acid — 50 mg	Zinc — 20 mg
B12 — 5 to 10 mcg	Iron — 10 mg for men;
	25 mg for women

When possible, we buy multi-vitamin-mineral capsules containing approximately these nutrients. It's far more economical than buying separate compounds. Then, in addition, each adult member of my family takes a gram of vitamin C (1000 mg) per day, increased to as much as 10 grams when colds and flu are going around.

Some people argue that taking more than the minimum daily requirement is a waste of money. However, research shows that environmental factors such as stress, chemical pollutants, and fatigue can vastly increase our needs for the so-called micronutrients. The B complex, for example, helps to restore the body's resistance to disease during times of stress. Vitamin C has been found to neutralize some of the effects of nitrites. Science has shown that zinc allows the human body to rid itself of mercury consumed in fish caught near industrial areas.

Of course, we all like to believe that knowledge of the effects of chemicals such as preservatives and herbicides is available and is, in some way, being applied in a sensible way by governmental regulating bodies. But this proves not to be the case. It is interesting to note, for example, that in a conference of the World Health Organization on "Pesticide Residues in Food," it was concluded that: "In the course of its deliberations on the toxicity and analysis of pesticide residues, the Joint Meeting has re-emphasized the importance of ascertaining the nature and amount of residues in food." And, in the paragraph directly following this one in the summary report, we learn that:

> In the course of its work, the FAO Working Party on Pesticide Residues frequently encountered gaps in information on world patterns of pesticide use, residues resulting from experimental programs, residues found in commerce, and losses of residues during storage and food processing.

Here is a partial list of pesticides studied by that group; all these pesticides are widely used in food production and processing:

Aldrin	Heptachlor
DDT	Methyl bromide
Gamma-BHC	Pyrethrins
Malathion	Carbaryl
Piperonyl butoxide	Ethylene dibromide
Dieldrin	Hydrogen phosphide
Diphenyl	Organic mercury compounds

On this list are some pesticides, such as DDT, which have been banned in the United States because it was demonstrated that they caused disease in humans — but which are still produced here and shipped to other countries for *their* use! Thus, even though we have passed legislation to protect ourselves from the dangers of DDT, we may still be eating foods contaminated with the stuff because we import foods grown in the countries where we still sell DDT.

Although we have, in the past fifty years, improved both production levels and world nutritional standards through the development of modern growing and processing methods, one wonders, at times, if it's been a fair trade-off. In recent years, researchers have even explored the area of irradiation as a means of destroying microorganisms in food products. This research seemed promising in its early phases — until it was proposed that irradiation could encourage the mutation of new microorganisms dangerous to humans and resistant to known methods of both control and detection.

In the past few years we've noticed a movement away from fast foods and convenience foods among still relatively small groups of people who are instead turning their attention to more healthy lifestyles. Home gardening and the use of organic foods are important in these movements. The alternatives—that is, of buying food grown without chemicals, or with a minimum of chemicals, or growing your own—are not, unfortunately, practical solutions for everyone. But there are other things we can do.

Many books have been written on the subject of providing highquality nutrition. Rather than report the work done, I'm going to recommend the following reading list:

> Dinaberg and Akel: *Nutrition Survival Kit: A Wholefoods Recipe and Reference Guide* (Panjandrum Press)
> La Buza: *Nutrition Crisis: A Reader* (West Publications)
> Watson: *Nutrition and Your Mind* (Bantam Books)
> Lappe: *Diet for a Small Planet* (Ballantine Books)
> Ebon: *Which Vitamin Do You Need?* (Bantam Books)
> Bricklin: *Natural Healing* (Rodale Press)
> Williams: *Nutrition Against Disease* (Bantam Books)

I do not necessarily mean that you should get all these books at once, but look over the ones you can find in your local bookstore and start with those that most attract you.

Environmental Factor Six: Stress

Dr. Hans Selye, a leading medical scientist exploring the problem of stress, showed that even "noxious stimuli" such as smells, dirt, and the like could set off dramatic physiological changes in animals. (Selye has described himself as "the first pharmacologist of dirt.") In fact, among these animals he demonstrated a reduction in the effectiveness of basic bodily defenses such as the lymph system and circulating lymphocytes. It is by this physiological dynamic that stress reduces our natural resistance to viral infections such as colds and the flu.

But what exactly is stress? Research has demonstrated that it is not simply the presence of pressure or threats, that is, stimuli from the outside, which creates stress. Rather, it is the person's (or animal's) inability to cope with that stimulus—say by altering it or escaping from it—that produces stress. Conflict and frustration immediately come to mind as synonyms for common stress experiences. It is a rare person indeed who does not experience stress—

conflict, indecision, frustration—almost daily in the modern world, either on the job or at home with the family. The degree of stress may be great or small, of course, but I'd venture to say that there is no one who has not experienced it.

What happens inside your body during stress is that your emotions rouse a gland known as the hypothalamus, which resides in your brain. That gland, in turn, sends messages to your pituitary gland. The pituitary then signals your adrenal glands—which send out hormones called glucocorticoids. The glucorcorticoids, which have important positive effects on the use of your large muscles, also cause your body to produce fewer antibodies and inhibit your body's ability to wall off infection.

Since that part of your brain which stimulates your hypothalamus is largely a visual center, your own powers to imagine—consciously as well as unconsciously—are responsible for setting off much of this complex response. Just as outside stimuli can influence you to produce threatening images you can also create images that are calming to you. Similarly, you can effect specific physiological responses in specific parts of your body.

Some people manifest stress as gastrointestinal disorders; others manifest it in respiratory problems, ranging in severity from the common cold to asthma. Your individual response to stress—that is, the way your personality responds to it—is believed to help determine what part of your body is likely to become the target of a disease. Thus a radio announcer who uses his or her oral capacities a lot, as opposed to a professional athlete whose main organs of expression are the large muscles, would be most prone to upper respiratory disease from this point of view.

The field of inquiry into personality types and how they match the kinds of diseases people get is a controversial one and extremely difficult to test. But I've found it interesting and fruitful to use oral imagery in a positive way for helping to keep sinus, throat, and nasal passages toned and relaxed. The following relaxation exercise, built on oral imagery, is one that I like to do:

Oral Images to Relax You

Bring a glass of water with you. Lie down in a place where you will not be disturbed for several minutes. Lie on your back, feet uncrossed, fingers resting on your rib cage.

Close your eyes. Let your jaw relax.

> Take a deep breath. Let it out slowly. Take another. Let it out slowly. And once more.
>
> Imagine yourself at the seashore, in a small cottage, where you can almost feel the movement of the waves rolling against the shore. You are warm, secure, at ease.
>
> Let your cheeks and facial muscles relax. Imagine invisible fingers lightly caressing the areas above and below your eyes and around your lips. If you wish to do so, lightly touch your face with your own fingertips. Then rest, enjoying the lingering tickling sensations as your face relaxes.
>
> Imagine that your whole body is turned to water, that you feel loose, heavy, and completely relaxed.
>
> Let yourself enjoy all these sensations for a few moments. Then get up slowly and languorously. Take a sip of cool water, hold it in your mouth, and let yourself enjoy these sensations also.
>
> Then let yourself ease back into your regular routines, enjoying the sensations of this exercise as long as you feel them.

From time to time throughout the day, you can pause for a moment and simply remember how it felt when you last did this relaxation exercise. The memory itself is a mini-version of the exercise and you'll be able to enjoy some of the same benefits through it.

Just as frightening images reduce the effectiveness of your immunological system, soothing, relaxing images signal your body to increase blood flow to every area of your body. Not only are antibody and walling-off responses restored, but the functions of blood and lymph, especially those of feeding and cleansing tissue, are actually stimulated.

Keep in mind that although we can't completely avoid stress in our lives we need not be victimized by it. Through self-structured relaxation we can direct our own inner healing abilities to return to a health-giving state. Learning to do this can be a major factor in building one's overall resistance to the viruses that cause colds and flu. Let's take a closer look at this.

Sometimes people experience areas of stress in their lives that seem not to get resolved from year to year although these people *are* seeking resolutions. And sometimes it's just difficult to locate the source of conflict causing the stress. In our work together Dr. Samuels and I have found that many people can begin to locate stress areas by devising a simple checklist. The list on the next page touches on most of the major activities in one's life. You may find it helpful to go through it to locate the areas where you can reduce stress in your life.

STRESS CHECKLIST

Job
☐ Do I feel satisfied in the kind of work I'm doing?
☐ Would I feel less stress if I did something to improve relationships with fellow workers?
☐ Can I improve my work area?
☐ Am I working too hard?
☐ Should I seek other employment?

Home
☐ Can I improve the place where I live?
☐ Do I need more space? Less space?
☐ Would I feel more relaxed if I rearranged my living spaces?
☐ Would I feel more relaxed if I spent more time with my family? Less time?
☐ Would I feel less stress if I resolved conflicts with my mate?

Privacy
☐ Would having more time alone help me relax?
☐ Are there things I want to do to feel more personal fulfillment in my leisure time?
☐ Would sitting down and getting to know myself help to reduce my stress?

Sleep
☐ Would improving sleep patterns make me more comfortable?
☐ Is there a time during the day when a few minutes' nap would help me relax?

Exercise
☐ Would taking a long walk in the morning, or after supper, help me relax more?
☐ Would taking up more vigorous exercise satisfy me in a way I'm now missing?

Diet
☐ Would eating alone, or in a calmer atmosphere, especially during my lunch break, reduce stress and help me enjoy my food more?
☐ Is my body stressed because I eat too much?
☐ Would foods other than those I'm now eating make my body feel better?

Sometimes, finding resolutions to stress stimuli can be made easier by working with other people. Most communities have resources for helping: group rap sessions, smoking clinics, dance therapy, yoga teachers, effectiveness training groups, parenting groups, vocational counselors, physical education groups, church counselors, sex and family counseling, and the like. Many communities have a "switchboard" — a phone number you can call to get names and addresses for these resources. The switchboard acts as a community referral service and is itself usually listed in the white pages of your phone book. If you have difficulty locating such a service, the nearest county social services department can tell you who to contact.

The following books offer further reading on the subject of stress, why it contributes to diseases, and how to reduce it in your life:

> Samuels and Bennett: *The Well Body Book* (Random House)
> Samuels and Bennett: *Be Well* (Random House)
> Samuels and Bennett: *Spirit Guides* (Random House)
> Samuels and Samuels: *Seeing with the Mind's Eye* (Random House)
> Mishra: *Fundamentals of Yoga* (Lancer Books)
> Geba: *Breathe Away Your Tensions* (Random House)
> Hurdle: *A Country Doctor's Common Sense Health Manual* (Parker)

SLEEP PATTERNS

In recent years researchers have experimented with both animals and humans in an attempt to discover the benefits of sleep. Research shows that when we sleep our bodies go into prolonged periods of deep relaxation during which certain healing processes, especially the healing of the mucosal tissue of your mouth and throat, go on at a far faster rate than while you're awake. Moreover, hormone balances change during sleep, increasing blood flow and the delivery of nutrients and antibodies to most organs of the body. A hormone known as "growth hormone," believed important to the regenerative processes, is found in measurable amounts in the adult only during sleep.

Few people have any doubts that sleep is important in preventing disease. Most of us have had the experience of getting colds or other infections more frequently when we are run down from lack of sleep than when we are rested and comfortable. Everyone's sleep patterns are different. Some people feel excellent with no more than four or five hours of sleep a day; others need eight or ten to experience the same feeling of well-being. However, there is a sleep pattern that most people follow regardless of the length of time they sleep: You go from light sleep to deep sleep and back to light sleep in ninety-minute cycles. During part of each cycle you go into a state of consciousness that researchers call REM, or rapid eye movement, sleep. This is when you dream.

Depriving people of just the REM cycle of sleep causes them to become moody, anxious, and depressed. During their waking hours people deprived in this way have difficulty concentrating, and they hallucinate. They may also experience radical shifts in appetite, eating either more or less than usual, and they become more susceptible to infection. Muscular coordination goes awry, vision blurs, and cardiovascular rhythms change from what is normal for those people.

If you don't think you sleep well, this may be an excellent place for you to begin your prevention program. When you wake up each morning, take a minute before rushing into your usual daily routine to ask yourself how you feel. If you feel well rested, wonderful! If you feel less than rested, ask yourself why. What is it that's disturbing your sleep?

Going to bed earlier than usual can solve sleep problems — because you then sleep longer and you begin your sleep before you've started feeling irritable and exhausted. Go to sleep when you feel comfortably drowsy, rather than after pushing yourself a couple hours past that point to finish work around the house or stay up for a late TV program.

Certain environmental factors can also be important to developing comfortable sleep patterns. Here's a bedroom checklist:

> Have a comfortable mattress.
> Have the room quiet.
> Make sure you are sleeping warmly but that the room is well ventilated.
> Even though the room is dark when you go to sleep at night, make sure that early morning lights aren't disturbing the end of your period of sleep.

If you find it hard to fall asleep at night, you'll probably discover that you can vastly improve the situation, and enjoy sleep more, by cutting down on stimulants: coffee, tea, cola drinks that contain caffeine, pep pills, and, when you've got a cold, cold pills. The latter can act as powerful stimulants for many people. Similarly, don't go to bed directly after eating a large meal or snack. Your stomach will not stop to rest until it has completed its work of digesting the food you've taken in, nor will you find yourself deep in sleep until this process is completed.

Drugs used to induce sleep can rob you of the necessary REM cycle. They also have side effects that work throughout your entire body and can reduce your natural resistance to disease. Most over-the-counter sleep preparations are nothing more than antihistamines, sometimes with aspirin or aspirin substitutes.

Light exercise such as an evening's walk around the block, or more strenuous exercise earlier in the day, will dramatically improve both your ability to fall asleep and the quality of your sleep during the entire cycle.

Resolving conflicts in your life that keep you awake is also essential. But recognize, also, that the relaxation exercises I describe in various parts of this book can be helpful to you in turning off occasional worries when you can't sleep. Having been an insomniac in the past, I think I can speak with personal authority on this point. I tried all the methods I've described before finally making changes in this dimension of my life. From this successful venture, I have this word of advice: Start with the simplest and most obvious causes of sleeplessness and then, if you find it necessary, work up to the more complex. I read numerous books on the subject, spent money on new mattresses and bedding, put more opaque shades on the window, and even went into psychotherapy to resolve deep-seated conflicts. I finally received wonderful, incredible, relaxing sleep by one simple change. I stopped drinking coffee!

People's tolerance to caffeine varies, but it's a powerful drug regardless of those tolerances. I had drunk two to four cups a day, not a lot by most people's estimates. But now I find that more than one full cup every few days noticeably affects my sleep.

Take your time exploring and discovering what changes in your life improve your enjoyment of sleep. Make changes at a comfortable pace, giving each one a week or more for your body to recognize the difference and adjust. Make your sleeping area an inviting, aesthetically pleasing space in your life, a place to which you'll truly enjoy going.

EXERCISE

In the past ten years Americans have begun to redefine the meaning of The Good Life. Jogging, cycling, swimming, and tennis, to say nothing of yoga, dance therapy, and weekly visits to the gym or spa, are replacing the habits of smoking, drinking, and eating foods rich in animal fats and sugars. The average American waistline gets slimmer as this trend continues, but for most people who enjoy a regular exercise program this is only a single aspect of the reward. The real benefits are sheer pleasure, a sense of well-being, and sometimes even euphoria, benefits that are truly profound.

Improved overall body toning means improved health and improved resistance to diseases such as colds and flu. The benefits to the person suffering from hypertension, or to the person who is interested in preventing certain of the most common heart diseases, or to the person being rehabilitated from a heart attack or stroke, have been well documented in the medical field. Less well known is the fact that with increased exercise your body produces more anti-bodies, it multiplies the numbers of freely circulating white blood cells to destroy bacteria, viruses, and cell debris, and it improves oxygen distribution throughout.

In *The New Aerobics,* Dr. Kenneth Cooper lists some of the benefits of exercise, both those documented by medical research and those established by firsthand experience of individuals or clinics:

> Improves bronchial and lung health by moving air in and out of the lungs more vigorously, thus toning the muscles of these areas, expanding lung capacity, and stimulating cilia activity
>
> Improves oxygen distribution in the tissues
>
> Improves the body's ability to handle sugars rather than storing them in fatty deposits
>
> Relieves anxiety and induces healthy fatigue, leading to comfortable sleep patterns.
>
> Dramatically improves self-image (which appears to be related both to hormonal changes and the sense of physical accomplishment)
>
> Reduces anxiety for people who are hypertense or experiencing emotional stress in their life
>
> Relieves migraine headaches
>
> Relieves arthritis in legs and back (although a few people complain that exercise aggravates these complaints)

All these benefits relate either directly or indirectly to the theme we've been discussing in this chapter — that of creating overall good health to prevent colds and the flu. Anyone still skeptical about exercise might consider the following statement by Dr. Cooper: "The whole field of exercise therapy is now in a state of transition from faddism to scientific legitimacy. Hardly a month passes without the publication of a significant new report on the numerous medical applications of exercise."

Starting an exercise program is not always easy, though, especially if you've been living a fairly sedentary existence for five years or more. Many people make the mistake of beginning with enthusiasm, overexerting, and then giving up after a week or two because they don't immediately feel super. Knowing that this is a common pattern, be warned. Look for an alternative that will allow you to enjoy the process in all its various stages.

Even after a short winter layoff, getting back into a regular exercise program works best if you go at it slowly. Begin with an evening's walk around the block. Do this for a week or two. Then map out a route of a mile and walk that. Enjoy the walk. Take pleasure in the things you see along the way. If you find a nagging little voice reminding you that this exercise stuff is "very serious business," ignore it. Ultimately, you will find yourself enjoying exercise and taking pleasure in the sensations of your body in a way offered by no other experience — except perhaps sexual experiences shared with a loved one. So if you must have a goal in this program, focus on enjoyment as your aim from the start. Let yourself enjoy each step along the way.

Gradually increase the briskness of your walk. After a couple weeks start jogging a part of the distance, doing what they call "intervals" — run awhile, walk awhile. Then, working at a pace that seems comfortable to you, increase your distances and times. Don't worry about competing with other people or with figures in a book. Trust your own feelings, and trust that the sense of physical and mental well-being you experience along the way is extremely important to your improved health.

I use walking and jogging as the example here, but the same underlying principles can be easily applied to sports such as swimming and bicycling. My own recommendation is that if you are just starting out in an exercise program, after either a winter's layoff or a number of sedentary years, don't go immediately into a competitive sport such as tennis, basketball, soccer, and the like. Give yourself time to become reacquainted with your body; and give your body time to make the necessary changes to enjoy these new activities.

Understanding that exercise is a growing process is important. We are not machines that can be turned on and off with the flip of a switch. We are much more than that. No matter what your age, healthy new growth occurs in your body as you begin an exercise program. As you make new demands on long unused muscle tissue, you begin growing hundreds of miles of new blood vessels to supply nutrients to the cells that make up the muscle tissue.

With exercise, cells change. The membranes become tougher, more elastic, and larger. As the outer surface of each healthy cell grows, it provides more area for extraction of oxygen and other nutrients from the bloodstream. Glandular responses also change. Even running around the block after a long layoff triggers a distress response in your body, a reaction that in medical terms is the same as a response to an emotionally charged confrontation—that is, a *stress* response. But after your body has grown up to the task, as it were, that long run is no longer a threat. On the contrary, the body responds with deep pleasure.

The most popular books on the subject of physical exercise, both how to get into it and what it does to improve your health, are the books on aerobics by Kenneth Cooper. Although there are other books around, Dr. Cooper's *The New Aerobics* is my favorite. I've never been in a bookstore where I didn't see this book, so it should be available in your neighborhood—maybe even on your drugstore or supermarket shelf.

REDEFINING DISEASE

In our book *Be Well*, Dr. Mike Samuels and I developed a program of prevention that begins by redefining the meaning of disease. Because of its value as a basic preventive tool I want to outline that program here, especially as it applies to upper respiratory health.

The word "disease" means, literally, lack of ease—that is, *dis-ease*. For most of us, disease is that point in our lives when we feel bad enough to want to stay home in bed. Where upper respiratory disease is concerned that usually means pain and fever: a sore throat, a stuffy nose, a headache, maybe even nausea or a slightly upset stomach. At the point when you are feeling these symptoms, you are probably in the middle stages of an upper respiratory infection and it is time to apply the kinds of remedies we looked at in Chapter Six. To take a preventive approach one obviously has to start long before this.

To represent this definition of disease, let's imagine a scale of ease and dis-ease that looks like this:

| Ease | | | | | | ↓ | | | | Dis-ease | |
| 1 | 2 | 3 | 4 | 5 | 6 | 7 | 8 | 9 | 10 | 11 | 12 |

The highest points in your life, when you feel exhilarated, vibrant, and free, are around 1 to 3 on the scale. Feelings of fever, depression, and pain, such as you might have with a bad flu infection, are around 10 or higher on the scale. On an average day, when things are just going along as usual, most people are in the 5 to 7 range.

Let's say that like most of us you do not consider yourself sick enough to do anything to help your body heal itself until you are around 8 to 10 on the scale; that is, you may not feel that you are sick enough to stop work and rest unless you have a headache, some fever, stuffy nose, and a sore throat. To use the ease/dis-ease scale, we recommend that you redefine the meaning of disease in your life by learning to pay attention to dis-ease in the 7 to 8 range. What does this mean in terms of colds and flu? It means that instead of changing your normal routine only when you have headache and fever (9 to 10 on the scale), you start changing when you have a slight throat tickle or tension in the back of your throat (7 or 8 on the scale).

By rescaling your definition of dis-ease, and learning to recognize more subtle symptoms than you presently do, you can begin the healing phase of a cold or flu before it becomes miserably uncomfortable or complicated by sinusitis or bacterial infection. And once you've learned to respond to your body's needs at the lower end of the scale, you will begin to suffer less and to reduce the number of days you are sick. Most people who've applied this tool in their lives have found that their body's natural healing abilities are able to stop the cold or flu before it becomes uncomfortable. What most people learn over a period of time working with this principle is that they can sometimes avoid the discomfort of colds entirely. They relax and rest while they still feel relatively good rather than when they are so uncomfortable they can barely stand themselves.

There are a number of techniques we recommend for incorporating this principle in your life—the first is to visualize the ease/dis-ease scale and then commit it to memory. Begin evaluating your general feelings, at different times of the day and over a period of a week or so, in terms of where they fall on the scale.

Establish a sense of your own middle ground on the scale. In other words, make note of how you feel on an average day — in the 5 to 7 range on the ease/dis-ease scale.

Once you establish your average feelings, start paying attention to the feelings you experience outside this range. Enjoy the lower end of the scale — that is, the ease end — and begin to look upon feelings on the higher end of the scale — the dis-ease end — as signals to change something in your life: to rest more, to develop relaxation techniques, to find out if your work environment is causing you problems, to stop smoking, to change your diet.

Dr. Samuels and I use what we call a "feeling pause" to make full use of the ease/dis-ease principle. The feeling pause is really very simple. You may already be doing it without realizing you are. The feeling pause is that moment when you briefly stop what you are doing, close your eyes for a second, sigh or yawn, and take stock of how you're feeling. Most people do this several times every day without realizing it.

My suggestion is to take this common experience, the feeling pause, and use the ease/dis-ease scale to evaluate what you're feeling. Sometimes it helps to establish the feeling pause in your mind as a clear and definite event. One way to embellish the feeling pause is to imagine yourself in a place where you feel particularly good. This might be at the beach, in the mountains skiing, or in a room at home where you feel especially at ease. Whenever you want to take a feeling pause, stop, briefly close your eyes, and imagine yourself being at that favorite place. For a moment just enjoy the daydream of the experience. Then recall the ease/dis-ease scale and evaluate how you've been feeling prior to taking the pause.

By structuring the feeling pause, and using it in this way to evaluate your feelings on the ease/dis-ease scale, you give yourself an important preventive tool. You learn to act sooner to help your body heal itself and you begin to trust your feelings of ease or dis-ease as signals for taking actions to create health.

AND THE NEXT STEP?

Probably as you were reading through this chapter you found yourself, like most people, more interested in some subjects than others. Follow that interest; see where it leads. It may show you where to begin improving specific aspects of your life—where to begin creating greater health and, therefore, resistance to colds, flu, or other diseases. Whether it was in stopping smoking, or reducing stress, or redefining your concept of disease, allow yourself to trust your interest as a compass in the wilderness.

Creating health, and therefore minimizing the discomforts of colds or the flu, is not something one does overnight or by reading one book. It is an ongoing creative venture. This is not to say that we should all stop everything else we're doing and focus only on this one concern. Far from it. I am a firm believer in the well-rounded life—work, play, conflict, tranquillity, sickness, health, to name just a few, all taken together, are essential ingredients for living a full and comfortable life.

However, as you allow yourself to become increasingly aware of the luxury of good health, of feeling really good, you find it more and more difficult to ignore whatever causes discomfort or dis-ease in life. Ideally, we find ourselves not only becoming less tolerant of these factors that run contrary to our ideas of health but also automatically seeking alternatives that will turn dis-ease to ease.

One need not become a health faddist or a fanatic to pursue these goals. More effective than faddists and fanatics, I believe, are people who are intelligent and well informed about their bodies and who enjoy ease (as distinguished from dis-ease) in their lives. Such people improve their own lives—and thus the quality of life around them—not by asking others to change but by actually making those changes for themselves now.

Creating health for oneself is really nowhere near as difficult as some faddists make it out to be. It is simply a matter of creating comfort in one's life, not just the more obvious comforts available through advanced technology and material well-being, though these can obviously be important, but comforts that come from experiencing more ease and pleasure with one's moment-to-moment existence—with living in the body-mind that is you.

For me, the greatest reward in learning about colds and flu has been in exploring ways to become more comfortable with my day-to-day, moment-to-moment existence. I want to feel comfortable in the body-mind which is my life, which is me. And the more I learn about the amazing capacities of my body the more I appreciate and enjoy it and the more I am able to do things that make my life more pleasurable.

I must confess that the moments of comfort and pleasure I most enjoy—probably because they are most accessible—are those when I feel at ease with myself, simply that, simply *ease*. Often these moments come unexpectedly: during a visit with a close friend, or while writing a paragraph in which the language seems to flow forth without effort, or during a quiet walk on a brisk fall morning. (My closer friends, I'm sure, might accuse me of making myself out as more contemplative than I really am if I didn't also mention that I thoroughly enjoy racing through the curves of a twisting mountain road on a fast motorcycle.)

The subtler moments of ease always surprise me when they come. Yet it is clear to me that the number of times I've experienced them has, through the years, increased as I have pursued the subject of health in the way we've explored it in this book. In this way, the study of common diseases such as colds and flu can truly transcend itself. I would find it gratifying to know that you, by reading this book, were able to enjoy some of the experiences of discovery that I've enjoyed while researching and writing it. For me, that would be one of those subtler moments of ease I've been talking about.

One last word: For anyone interested in pursuing some of the ideas we've discussed in this book, take a look at the annotated reading list on page 147.

Be well!

References

Walter McQuade and Ann Aikman: *Stress* (New York: Bantam, 1975).
P.W. Sheehan (ed.): *The Function and Nature of Imagery* (New York: Academic Press, 1972).
Mike Samuels, M.D., and Nancy Samuels: *Seeing with the Mind's Eye* (New York: Random House, 1975).
E.D. Wittkower, M.D., and R.A. Cleghorn, M.D.: *Recent Developments in Psychosomatic Medicine* (Philadelphia: Lippincott, 1958).
Mike Samuels, M.D., and Hal Z. Bennett: *Be Well* (New York: Random House, 1975).
S.M. Fox and W.L. Hasket: "Physical Activity and the Prevention of Coronary Heart Disease," *Bulletin of the New York Academy of Medicine* (August, 1968).
Arthur C. Guyton: *Medical Physiology* (Philadelphia: Saunders, 1976).
Kenneth Cooper, M.D.: *The New Aerobics* (New York: Bantam, 1970).

Sir Charles H. Stuart-Harris and Geoffrey C. Schild: *Influenza: The Viruses and the Disease* (Littleton, Mass.: Publishing Sciences Group, 1976).

Edwin D. Kilbourne (ed.): *The Influenza Viruses and Influenza* (New York: Academic Press, 1975).

World Health Organization: Technical Report Series 370.

World Health Organization: *The Technical Basis for Legislation on Irradiated Food*. Technical Report 316.

Hans Selye: *Stress* (Montreal: Acta, 1950).

Conference of the Society for Psychosomatic Research: *Stress Disorder* (Springfield, Ill.: Charles C Thomas, 1958).

Appendix

Reading List

Allergy Information Association: Room 7, Poynter Drive, Weston, Ontario, M9R 1L1. This Canadian group is an important resource center for all kinds of allergies. They publish well-written, inexpensive pamphlets, as well as a quarterly newsletter. Write to them for a complete list of their services.

Be Well: Mike Samuels, M.D., and Hal Z. Bennett (New York: Random House, 1975). In this book Dr. Samuels and I describe a new way to evaluate disease, so that you can take action to make yourself well long before symptoms necessitating a doctor's help become apparent.

A Country Doctor's Common Sense Health Manual: J. Frank Hurdle, M.D. (New York: Parker, 1975). This is one of my favorite home medical handbooks. Though it is not as comprehensive as *The Well Body Book,* this book gives solid information, based on the author's many years of clinical experience, for changing specific areas in your life that contribute to disease. Has a particularly good section on colds. Much of Dr. Hurdle's work is based on his observation that stress is a major cause of disease. His cures work because the patient makes an active choice to improve his or her life. Uses a case history approach to explain disease and the healing process. Although this book is not easily available, it is well worth ordering from your local bookstore.

The Doctor's and Patient's Handbook of Medicine and Drugs: Peter Parrish, M.D. (New York: Knopf, 1977). A comprehensive, well-written guide to the use, effects, and side effects of the principal prescription and nonprescription remedies.

Finger Acupressure: Pedro Chan (New York: Ballantine, 1975). Based on the principles of acupuncture, finger acupressure can be used by everyone to reduce the muscular tension and pain which is caused by stress. Good how-to material with photos and verbal descriptions to help you. A brief foreword, written by an M.D., presents an overview of acupuncture and acupressure in their medical applications.

Fundamentals of Yoga: Rammurti Mishra, M.D. (New York: Lancer, 1959). This amazing book, written by a medical doctor, provides good information about what yoga does and how you can do it. Grounded in modern endocrinology, the book is easy to read and free of medical jargon, though it goes into detail about the relationships between yoga and the glandular functions of your body.

Government Guides to Health and Nutrition: Ralph L. Woods, ed. (New York: Pyramid, 1975). The editor has put together a catalog, with short reviews, of books and pamphlets about health, all available from the Government Printing Office. Even though getting material from the GPO has become almost like pulling teeth, some of the material they offer is worth the wait. If you have the patience to deal with this often aggravating bureaucracy, it is a good way to start your home medical library inexpensively.

A Guide to Alternative Medicine: Donald Law (New York: Dolphin, 1976). The author examines sixty different forms of healing. The first part of the book contains a thought-provoking history and philosophy addressed to the question "What is healing?"

Medical Self-Care: Box 717, Inverness, California 94937. This quarterly magazine reviews self-help medical materials and contains articles about basic paramedical skills, prevention, how to use your local medical library, and so forth. An excellent periodical, fathered by a Yale medical student. You can get a sample copy by sending $2 to the publisher.

Natural Healing: Mark Bricklin (Emmaus, Pa.: Rodale Press, 1976). This very interesting book is actually a collection of articles, arranged like an encyclopedia, on subjects ranging from Acne to Yoga. Put together by the editor of *Prevention* magazine, its list of contributors includes medical doctors, biochemists, herbalists, and nutrition experts. A short section on the human body's natural healing abilities, written by Alan Bricklin, M.D., makes the book well worth the $12.95 price tag.

The New Aerobics: Kenneth Cooper, M.D. (New York: Bantam, 1970). Aerobics is physical exercise that raises your physical capacities to a level which strengthens heart, lungs, and blood vessels and improves your overall toning and self-image. Dr. Cooper's book is the bible on the subject. A practical how-to book with easy to understand medical groundwork.

A New Self: Muriel James and Louis M. Savary (Reading, Mass.: Addison-Wesley, 1977). This book helps you get in touch with areas of your life that may be causing conflict, and it describes effective techniques for reducing the stress which arises from those conflicts. Uses transactional analysis techniques and gives solid support for making decisions about ways to improve your life and reduce stress.

Nutrition Against Disease: Roger J. Williams, M.D. (New York: Bantam, 1973). A world-renowned leader in vitamin research, Dr. Williams is a biochemist who has contributed much to our understanding of vitamins and minerals. A sound, solidly based book about how vitamins and minerals work in your body to create health.

Nutrition Survival Kit: Kathy Dinaberg and D'Ann Akel (San Francisco: Panjandrum Press, 1976). Tells you virtually everything you need to know about food, the nutritional content of food, and the best way to prepare it. Contains delicious recipes.

Seeing with the Mind's Eye: Mike Samuels, M.D., and Nancy Samuels (New York: Random House, 1975). In this book, Dr. Samuels and his wife explore the power of the human mind to visualize. All aspects are examined — from the creation of art to the creation of health. Full-color plates and explanatory drawings complement the text by providing a solid presentation of this important human capacity. I include this book here because I believe that understanding this wonderful human skill is essential for making changes in one's life to create health.

Stress: Walter McQuade and Ann Aikman (New York: Bantam, 1975). In an easy-to-understand style, the authors tell you both the emotional and the physical basis of stress. Though technical in its roots, the language is simple, and some of the information will truly surprise you. Among other things, it discusses stress and resistance to disease. Has how-to material for reducing stress.

The Well Body Book: Mike Samuels, M.D., and Hal Z. Bennett (New York: Random House, 1973). In this book Dr. Samuels and I present what has become a basic home medical handbook, as well as a framework for what has become known as holistic medicine. Here is a system of home medicine that is not simply a translation of common medical practices, but one that is designed from the bottom up for self-care. Contains a large diagnosis and treatment section, a prevention section, and alternative healing techniques that really work. Demystifies doctors and creates a new way to approach disease and healing.

Index of Ailments

Index of Remedies

Index